LIVING, LEARNING, AND LANGUAGING ACROSS BORDERS

Addressing the roles of education, language, and identity in cyclical migration, this book highlights the voices and experiences of transborder students in Mexico who were born or raised in the US. The stories develop a portrait of the lived realities, joys, and challenges that young people face across elementary, secondary, and tertiary levels.

The book not only discusses migration and education policies and pedagogies grounded in the fluid lives of these young people, but its photography also presents their experiences in a visual dimension that words alone cannot capture. This in-depth, multimodal study examines the interplay of language, power, and schooling as they affect students and their families to provide insights for educators to develop meaningful pedagogies that are responsive to students' border crossing experiences.

Living, Learning, and Languaging Across Borders is a vital resource for pre- and in-service teachers, teacher educators, graduate students and scholars in bilingual and multilingual education, literacy and language policy, and immigration and education in the US, Mexico, and beyond. It offers important insights into the complex landscapes transborder students navigate, and considers policy and pedagogy implications that reject problematic assumptions and humanize approaches to the education and migration experiences of transborder students.

Tatyana Kleyn is Associate Professor and Director of the Bilingual Education and TESOL Programs at The City College of New York, USA.

Tim Porter is a photographer and journalist who has worked for a variety of newspapers as a reporter and editor.

LIVING, LEARNING, AND LANGUAGING ACROSS BORDERS

Students Between the US and Mexico

Tatyana Kleyn
Photography by Tim Porter

NEW YORK AND LONDON

First published 2022
by Routledge
605 Third Avenue, New York, NY 10158

and by Routledge
2 Park Square, Milton Park, Abingdon, Oxon OX14 4RN

Routledge is an imprint of the Taylor & Francis Group, an informa business

© 2022 Taylor & Francis

The right of Tatyana Kleyn and Tim Porter to be identified as authors of this work has been asserted by them in accordance with sections 77 and 78 of the Copyright, Designs and Patents Act 1988.

All rights reserved. No part of this book may be reprinted or reproduced or utilised in any form or by any electronic, mechanical, or other means, now known or hereafter invented, including photocopying and recording, or in any information storage or retrieval system, without permission in writing from the publishers.

Trademark notice: Product or corporate names may be trademarks or registered trademarks, and are used only for identification and explanation without intent to infringe.

Library of Congress Cataloging-in-Publication Data
A catalog record for this title has been requested

ISBN: 978-0-367-35547-0 (hbk)
ISBN: 978-0-367-35546-3 (pbk)
ISBN: 978-0-429-34017-8 (ebk)

DOI: 10.4324/9780429340178

Typeset in Bembo
by Taylor & Francis Books

To all the transborder students de aquí, allá y más allá

CONTENTS

Acknowledgements	*ix*
Author and Photographer Biographies	*xiv*
Foreword	*xvi*
Preface	*xx*

PART I
Overview of Cyclical Migration   **1**

1	Return Migration in Context: Policies, Demographics, and Terminology	3
2	Transborder Students and Families	21
3	Family Return to Mexico	45

PART II
Issues Impacting Students   **61**

4	Shifting National Identities and Immigration Statuses	63
5	Language Learning, Unlearning, and Relearning	88
6	Two Countries, One Education	110

viii Contents

PART III
Lessons Learned 139

7 Policy and Pedagogy Implications 141

Epilogue: Where Are They Now? 161

Index *167*

ACKNOWLEDGEMENTS

In the eight years this book has gone from conceptualization to publication, many, many people across the US and Mexico have supported this undertaking. First and foremost, I express my deepest gratitude, respect y cariño to the students and families who generously invited me into their homes, schools, and dreams. Mi agradecimiento eterno a cada uno de ustedes, por permitirme entrar a sus vidas y confiar en mí para capturar sus experiencias y compartir sus historias en este libro y en la película. A todes ustedes mis más sinceras diozkilln luuy, gracias, спасибё, and thank you. Your experiences, strength, and resilience help us imagine a world that is, like your lives, beyond borders.

I was extraordinarily fortunate to cross paths with my now friend and collaborator, Tim Porter, when I was in Oaxaca. Tim is not only a photographer whose images take your breath away, he is also a colleague who has gone above and beyond in editing my writing and pushing my ideas. Thank you, Jody Noble, for connecting us!

Yauzin Adalid Martínez García has shaped this work more than anyone. I was introduced to Yauzin, then a transborder student at la Universidad Autónoma Benito Juárez de Oaxaca (UABJO), over email prior to arriving in Oaxaca. We got on a Skype call and after a brief conversation I immediately asked her not only to be a participant in the study, but to be my research assistant too. Thankfully she agreed and has worked with me on all aspects of this study. Xquixe pe lii, Yauzin.

Not everyone has that special someone who they can always count on, but I am beyond fortunate to have that in Nancy Stern. Although I refer to her as my very critical friend, she is so much more. I cannot even begin to thank her for all the time she has spent talking through emerging ideas, reading, editing, and rereading sections of the book I was struggling with, and just being an overall support system in this and every other aspect of my life.

x Acknowledgements

My time in Oaxaca was immeasurably influenced by my fellow Fulbrighters in 2014–2015. I had the great fortune to learn from and with William Perez and Rafael Vásquez as collaborators on the *Una Vida, Dos Países* film; Ronda Brulotte became my Libres roommate and guide in figuring out life in Oaxaca; and Alexandra Délano who I had to go all the way to Mexico to meet so we could continue to be colleagues in New York! I am forever grateful that all our trajectories led us to the same place at the same time.

Before I headed to Oaxaca I was told by numerous people that I needed to meet Mario López-Gopar. They were all right. Mario immediately welcomed me to the UABJO and the Facultad de Idiomas (Faculty of Languages). He invited me to speak to his class—which on that day was briefly interrupted by an earthquake alarm—and has consistently been a source of support, information, and inspiration. UABJO faculty and leaders Bill Sughrua, Edwin Nazaret León Jiménez and Fernando Martínez Sánchez also welcomed and supported me from day one. The UABJO became my second academic home, where I had the good fortune to teach a wonderful group of graduate students who have since become my friends. I appreciate Nicasio Martinez Miguel, who has answered my non-stop questions about Diidx zah. Flor Ordoñez-Vilches, Luisa Eliet Arellanes Cancino, María de la Paz Vásquez Méndez, Mónica Robles Romero, Yareni Elizabeth Sánchez Cantán, and Yesenia Bautista Ortiz; thank you for accompanying me on this journey.

I never imagined that an apartment building I stumbled upon in the Centro would lead me to the most special people. Lola Newell, who (literally) opened the gates to Libres was a constant sounding board during my time in Oaxaca and beyond. Estela Nolasco me acogió en su hogar sin casi conocerme. Y se ha convertido en una amiga muy especial que me ha ayudado a realmente entender lo que significa "¡Oaxaca, tienes que vivirlo!" Peggy Fisher del Bosque is another friend who has supported this project from its inception. I also appreciate the collaboration and conversations with Deek Keis, an educator, photographer, and friend.

Llegar a una comunidad como una extraña que viene a hacer investigación, especialmente sobre migración, siempre es complicado. Sin embargo, tuve la fortuna de encontrar educadores que me abrieron las puertas y confiaron en mi trabajo con sus estudiantes. En el Centro de Estudios Tecnológicos y de Servicios 124 (CETis 124) de Tlacolula no pude haber encontrado mejores colaboradores que el Dr. Marco Antonio Pereyra Rito y el Lic. Abisaí Aparicio García. Ellos no solo me dieron la bienvenida a su escuela, sino que hicieron lo mismo con mis alumnos de City University of New York (CUNY) y pusieron mucho esfuerzo en el lanzamiento del documental *Una Vida, Dos Países* y la guía de apoyo a docentes con estudiantes transfronterizos en México. También estoy agradecida con el Mtro. Salvador Fuentes Pineda, Lic. Salvador Jiménez Andrade, Lic. Juan Azamar García, Mtro. Efraín Luis Hernández, Lic. Leticia Pérez Hernández y Mtra. Itandi Flores Cruz por darme la bienvenida al CETis 124.

Estoy muy agradecida con Elizabeth Arellanes Vicente quien me presentó a las familias transfronterizas en la Ciénega de Zimatlán y me abrió las puertas de su hermoso hogar. Mis viajes a Oaxaca no son lo mismo sin comprar vestidos de la región del Istmo con Elizabeth.

My Teachers College (TC) connections Tori Hunt, Kate Menken, and Mary Mendenhall, now decades in the making since our lives intersected on 120th Street, are an essential and wonderful part of both my professional and personal life. My learning at TC was under the mentorship of María Torres-Guzmán, who I carry with me in all I do. Although I met Ofelia García at TC, it was CUNY that brought us together. Through our treasured collaborations I have learned to be a better teacher and researcher, and how to do it from the heart.

Many years ago I found my academic home at the City College of New York (CCNY) and I've never looked back. I am immensely grateful for the support of our current President Vince Boudreau, former President Lisa Staiano-Coico and School of Education Dean Edwin Lamboy, and I'm appreciative of the collegiality of my CCNY colleagues. I am thankful to the US-Mexico Foundation and the Jaime Lucero Mexican Studies Institute at CUNY. This work has been supported by my 2014–2015 fellowship leave, a research award from my union, PSC-CUNY, and the Fulbright Program, which made this research possible.

I am fortunate to have CUNY frolleagues (friends who are colleagues) who make work enjoyable: Dina López, Carmina Markar, Ariana Mangual Figueroa, Marit Dewhurst, Sobha Kavanakudiyil, and my immigration co-teachers in law and psychology, Stephanie Delia and Adeyinka Akinsulure-Smith. One of the best parts about being at CUNY is our students, including those I have met in my classes and through the CCNY Dream Team. I am grateful to Amalia Oliva Rojas, Antonio Alarcón, Areli Morales, Ashley Busone Rodríguez, Emmanuel Vilchis, Farah Shawkat, Guadalupe Vidal Martinez, Irma Cruz, Irving Mota, Isabel Mendoza-García, Jaqueline Cinto-Lozano, Kellie Griffith, Nancy, Roxana, Saulo Jimenez-Reyes, Vanessa, and Yatziri Tovar Campos who have been my students, but are equally if not more so my teachers, and have become friends and collaborators.

I have been fortunate to work in community and in familia with amazing people who have created spaces to cultivate this work. I am forever grateful and proud to be part of the CUNY Initiative on Immigration and Education (CUNY-IIE), CUNY New York State Initiative on Emergent Bilinguals (CUNY-NYSIEB), Dos Puentes Elementary School, the New York State Association for Bilingual Education (NYSABE), and the Multilingual Learner Project (MLP). Leza Rawlins deserves special mention for always providing assistance on multiple fronts.

Many committed people do important work illuminating the experiences of immigrants across the globe including those who live between the US and Mexico, and I am grateful to learn from and with them: Daniela Alulema Jill Anderson, Eric Bybee, Cynthia Carvajal, Colette Despagne, Ben Donnellon, Sarah Gallo, Patricia Gándara, Ted Hamann, Bryant Jensen, Jong-Min, Maggie Loredo, M, Maru Ponce, Rosario Quiroz Villarreal, Liz Robbins, Betstabé Román, Juan Sánchez García, and Víctor Zúñiga, among others who have paved the way in this field.

xii Acknowledgements

Writing for me is always hard, but writing during a pandemic has been especially challenging. I don't know how I would have gotten through this without the peer accountability and support of Maite T. Sánchez and Sara Vogel, the founding members of our online writing group. I am also thankful to my yoga teachers—Anna Haddad and Alosja van Leeuwen—for helping me clear my mind when the world was in a state of chaos. Namaste.

I have relied on the encouragement and support of so many friends: Cristina Salazar, Dina Goldstein Silverman, Nancy Villarreal de Adler, Tamara Alsace, Carmen Dinos, Claire Sylvan, Angelo Cabrera, Rebeca Madrigal, Moira Wilkinson, Yennifer Pinales, and my BFF since age five, Keren Ray, and Angela Paredes who provided professional translation support of the highest caliber and counted me down to the book's completion.

It was the memories of my own experiences crossing borders as a child that led me to this work. I am forever grateful to my family for their unconditional love: my mother, Fanya Mozeshtam, for being the force to motivate our family to migrate and a model of hard work and perseverance, and my father, Jack Kleyn, who offered me space with warm sunshine as I finished writing this book away from the freezing New York City winter. My sister and brother-in-law, Beth and Ray Wushenker, have cheered me on every step of the way.

Thank you to Karen Adler, my editor at Routledge, for her flexibility and commitment to this project. Finally, my deep gratitude to Karen Zaino, who has asked critical questions all along the way, and has edited nearly every word of this book. I am thrilled that it has come to completion and hope that it does justice to the transborder students and families it features.

Tatyana Kleyn

More than anyone, I thank the families in Oaxaca who opened their lives to me, who trusted me with their words and with their stories, and who welcomed me into their homes and invited me to birthday parties, weddings, and graduations. I met them as an *extranjero,* an immigrant in their culture; they embraced me as a friend. Meeting them, knowing them, and photographing them is one of the great gifts of my life. I am honored to know them, and humbled by their friendship.

I began photographing seriously in Oaxaca after meeting Mary Ellen Mark, the late documentary photographer, at a workshop there. Mary Ellen was an extraordinary soul who believed in the power of a single image to convey the complexities of humanity. "I'm just interested in people on the edges," she once said. "I feel an affinity for people who haven't had the best breaks in society ... I find them more human maybe. What I want to do more than anything is acknowledge their existence." I carry these words with me when I photograph in Oaxaca. Mary Ellen urged me to return again and again to the people I photograph, to keep looking for the universal amid the quotidian. She inspired me to see deeper, to take risks, both photographically and culturally, and to seek authenticity in my work. "Photograph the world as it is," she said. "Nothing is more interesting than reality." In the short time we knew each other, Mary Ellen changed my life. My photography displays the gratitude I have for her.

Tatyana Kleyn is the driving force behind this book, intellectually and emotionally. My contribution would not have happened had she not asked me to participate in a small way during her initial research in Oaxaca. She, like the families, trusted me, and for that confidence I am forever grateful.

Tatyana and I met through a mutual friend, Jody Noble. I am indebted to her for the introduction, which triggered our collaboration. Of such random encounters life is made.

Finally, I would not have known Oaxaca had my wife, KT, in the years before our marriage, not enticed me to travel with her to this magical, complicated place. She had studied Spanish there as a teenager and wanted Oaxaca to be a part of our life. Eventually, we married in Oaxaca, in the home of her god-parents, and built our own house there. When I began to pursue journalistic and documentary interests in Oaxaca, she was relentless in her encouragement. Her reward, she says, is our deepening involvement in an ever-widening circle of Oaxacan life. As she is apt to say, she introduced me to Oaxaca, and I, through my photography, reintroduced her to it.

Tim Porter

AUTHOR AND PHOTOGRAPHER BIOGRAPHIES

Tatyana Kleyn is Associate Professor and Director of the Bilingual Education and TESOL Programs at The City College of New York. She received an Ed. D. from Teachers College, Columbia University in International Educational Development with a focus in Bilingual/Bicultural Education. Tatyana is Principal Investigator for CUNY-IIE. She served as president of the New York State Association for Bilingual Education and was a Fulbright Scholar in Oaxaca, Mexico. Tatyana has authored books and articles on immigration, translanguaging, and bilingual education. Her work in film as a producer and director includes the *Living Undocumented* series, *Una Vida, Dos Países: Children and Youth (Back) in Mexico*, and the *Supporting Immigrants in Schools* video series. Tatyana was an elementary school teacher in San Pedro Sula, Honduras and Atlanta, Georgia.

Website: www.TatyanaKleyn.com

Tim Porter is a photographer and journalist who has worked for a variety of newspapers as a reporter and editor, including the Hearst-owned *San Francisco Examiner*, where he was the assistant managing editor for news and founding editor of the newspaper's web operation. Tim has freelanced as a writer and as a photographer for institutions and publications such as the University of California, the John S. and James L. Knight Foundation, and *Marin Magazine*, where he was principal photographer for eight years. Since 2013, Tim has concentrated on documentary photography in Oaxaca, Mexico, working with families who have returned to their towns of origin from the United States, single mothers and their children, and other marginalized communities. His work was featured in 2017 at the Centro Fotográfico Manuel Álvarez Bravo in Oaxaca.

Website: www.photography.timporter.com

FOREWORD

As a research team, our joint work began 20 years ago as we first wondered about where Mexican newcomer students who left their new school districts in the United States went when they moved on. We hypothesized that perhaps some moved/returned with their families to Mexico and in 2004 began a Consejo Nacional de Ciencia y Tecnología (CONACYT), a supported study in two of Mexico's traditional "sending states"—one a high-volume participant in transnational migration (Zacatecas) and one that has long generated a more modest volume (Nuevo León). What we did not know then was that the phenomenon we were examining was about to grow substantially larger in scale and would encompass practically every state and region in Mexico, including Oaxaca, the focal Mexican state for this volume.

Recent Mexican census tallies suggest there are 600,000 children and youth of the qualifying ages for *educación básica* (which spans three years of *kinder* for 3- to 6-year-olds, six years of *primaria* for 6- to 12-year-olds, and three years of *secundaria* for 12- to 15-year-olds) who were born in the United States (Masferrer et al., 2019). Those data also point to US-born students in Mexican high schools (*preparatoria*) and in the traditional age-range for college. Many of those started school in the US before moving to Mexico. Less well tallied by the Mexican Census and schools, which note birthplace, but clear from our survey research across now five Mexican states (adding Puebla, Jalisco, and Morelos), there are several hundred thousand additional children and youth in Mexican schools who were born in Mexico, moved to the US, and have moved back.

Sharing numbers, as we do above, is important, as it clarifies the scale of the phenomenon and the need for educational policy responses (e.g., teacher professional development or curricular adaptations related to welcoming those with school experience elsewhere; Hamann, 2021). Similarly, pointing out that these transnational students are in Mexico under different circumstances (e.g., some with citizenship rights in the US based on US birthplace and others not having that status), hints at the heterogeneity of this population. But numbers alone are not vivid. They do not highlight the variously fraught, difficult, and transcendent experiences of children and youth who have moved as part of the largest migration between two countries in the world (i.e., the back and forth between the US and Mexico). They do not illuminate the negotiation of schools and communities in two nations that these young people have had to pursue. That's where this evocative and substantial new volume by Tatyana Kleyn and photographer Tim Porter becomes so powerful and important.

While first tracing the same larger social dynamics that our work has examined, the focus (and quite literally the camera lens) quickly turn here to nine "transborder students" (to use Kleyn's preferred terminology) and, in softer focus, their families and educators. This, in turn, replaces numbers with Axianeydt, Yauzin, Karla, Melany, Sharely, Erik, Brayan, Melchor, and Ricardo. It also goes beyond any of our work by including students at the high school and university levels.

The volume gets both more humane and more humanities-oriented with the inclusion of poetry, artwork, and Porter's spare and respectful black and white photographs. Not only are we as readers and viewers positioned to contemplate the photos, so too were the focal children and youth using a technique called photo-elicitation. They and their families reviewed the photos, identified their favorites, and clarified ideas and memories that the images evoked. Individually and cumulatively the photographs succeed at moving us further away from numbers and even labels like "transborder students" that flatten or strip away detail and nuance from agentive, complicated, uniquely circumstanced individuals. In all instances the negotiation of school and community in two countries is by a person, not a kind of person. That person is part of a unique network of family, peers, educators, and others. Although we sometimes need to ignore some particularities to shape policies for those in similar but not synonymous circumstances, we always lose a bit when we accept such reductions, such blurring. Kleyn and Porter push insistently against such reductiveness.

The photographic images and text here create an opportunity to broaden readers' perspectives towards the varied lived realities of transborder youth and in Kleyn's case show a continuation of her use of multiple media to promote understanding. This volume updates and substantially complements the insights that are also compellingly shared in the short documentary she co-produced with William Pérez and Rafael Vásquez, *Una Vida, Dos Países* (www.unavidathefilm.com/#watch-the-film), a 30-minute documentary from 2016 that we recommend readers watch before, during, or after they consider these pages.

While this book is centrally and obviously about transborder youth, after an evocative, consistently translanguaging poem as its lengthy epigraph, the opening sentence of Chapter 1 declares a higher purpose and higher premise than just the account of these focal nine young people and their border spanning families and educational networks. The chapter starts, "Imagine a world where people are truly free." It later continues, "A truly free world is one where borders are either inexistent or permeable, used to distinguish one politically administrative location from another, but not to mandate who belongs and benefits and who is left on the periphery." After we have made our way through the subsequent six chapters and an epilogue (including quotations like that of Emanuel, a transborder parent, in Chapter 3, explicitly naming the need to be "free"), the reason for this sweeping start becomes more obvious. We, meaning we the readers, are being told these accounts, shown these images, and asked to understand these transborder youth's circumstances because we are expected to become contributors to the work of making a better, more free world. Most of the readers of this volume will be from the US or Mexico, but more than a few will identify with both countries and will concur that there can be richness and possibility in growing up in more than one place, in learning and mastering more than one system, in being able to outflank forces of subordination and stratification. But the fact that all this is possible does not mean that contemporarily much of this is so.

This book briefly welcomes us into the worlds of nine young people, currently in Mexico, previously in the United States. It asks us to better understand them through their stirring words about their homes and dreams, like in Chapter 4, when Sharely talked about her handprint and the stars she drew in the cement of the bedroom that her father was adding to their home in Oaxaca, an image shared directly with the reader in an accompanying photograph. She explains:

> When I see [the photograph], I feel like I am home. Because it is my home. The handprint has my name and my sister's name. It is mine. My property. No one could take my home away. I would write beneath it: A home of ours. It's like I leave my handprint here in Mexico. It's where I am. The star is because of all the stars in Mexico. You can see the stars here very well because there are not a lot of buildings or light. We have the stars—one point for Mexico.

Indeed, one point for Mexico.

While we feel we have learned a lot from our own studies of transborder students, this book teaches us much more. We are to be troubled by quotes, like the epigram from Yauzin that starts Chapter 6: "My first motivation to come back was to continue my studies and the second was racism." It asks to consider ways schools in Mexico and the US could be more welcoming of and responsive to transborder students. It asks to consider transnational as well as national policy and immigration enforcement policy as well as education policy. Throughout we are asked to question barriers and, in parlance that might sound like a Reaganesque rejoinder to the former Trump administration, we are beseeched to "tear down walls." So, for the sake of transborder students, their families, and all of us, let's do that. There's work to do.

Edmund "Ted" Hamann
University of Nebraska–Lincoln, USA
Víctor Zúñiga
Tecnológico de Monterrey, Mexico
Juan Sánchez García
Escuela Normal Miguel F. Martínez, Monterrey, Mexico

References

Hamann, E. T. (2021). Las implicaciones de la migración transnacional entre Estados Unidos / México para el desarrollo profesional de los docentes: perspectivas antropológicas. *Anales de Antropólogia*, 55(1): 107–116.

Masferrer, C., Hamilton, E. R., & Denier, N. (2019). Immigrants in their parental homeland: Half a million U.S.-born minors settle throughout Mexico. *Demography*, 56, 1453–1461.

PREFACE

Immigration for me is an area of both personal and professional interest. When I was almost six, my family left the Soviet Union from what is now Latvia for the United States. We were fleeing from anti-Semitism, and as Jews we were able to receive political refugee status. We were sponsored by the Hebrew Immigrant Aid Society (HIAS), a humanitarian organization created by US Jews to aid Jewish refugees that now works with refugees and asylum seekers from all over the world. HIAS provided myriad services for my family and the thousands of others who came to the US under similar circumstances. The organization paid for our flight to Columbus, Ohio, our resettlement community (we eventually repaid them). They picked us up from the airport and took us to our apartments, one for my grandparents and another for my parents and myself—a shocking and welcome surprise. In the Soviet Union we all shared one apartment along with another family. HIAS helped us get settled, took us to the grocery store, and enrolled my parents and grandparents in English classes. This support was critical in setting up my family for success as we started our new lives in the US, where we eventually became naturalized citizens.

Two decades later I was fortunate to be a professor of Bilingual Education and Teaching English to Speakers of Languages Other than English (TESOL) at The City College of New York (CCNY). The university is located in Washington Heights—perhaps best known for the Broadway show and movie *In the Heights*—and is home to the largest Dominican community in the US. There I have met many amazing students, the majority of them immigrants from the Dominican Republic, Mexico, and China, who were studying to become bilingual teachers and teachers of English as a new language (ENL) in New York City and beyond. As we developed trusting relationships, I learned that some were undocumented. They were exhausted from being on guard constantly, they feared that if they were not "perfect" they would run into trouble with law enforcement, and they were uncertain about whether they would ever attain teaching positions without a Social Security number (some were eventually able to teach through the DACA program). I began to see firsthand how being an immigrant is not a singular or even similar experience. As refugees, my family and I had foundational supports that most immigrants, and especially undocumented immigrants, do not receive. My undocumented students not only received zero support, they have had hurdles thrown in front of them at every turn. These obstacles affect their ability to study, work, drive, and feel safe. These contrasting experiences have led me to work more closely with undocumented students at CCNY as I learned how their families struggled in their home countries just as mine did within a context of anti-Semitism. I saw them as targets of political decisions that determine whose suffering warrants entry into the US and whose does not. These government actions have barred them from being fully accepted and integrated into the nation (Patel, 2015).

This study emerged in an era of heated and highly politicized disagreements around US deportation practice in the 2010s. During that time and the preceding years, immigrant rights activists labeled then President Barack Obama the "Deporter-In-Chief." Immigration was, and continues to be, a contentious national and transnational issue, and a frequent topic of debate across media platforms. Personally, I was always struck by the constant splaying across the news of rising deportation statistics and the absence of accompanying stories about the affected people. Deportation became numbers on a graph; the human impact was ignored. Meanwhile, as part of an immigrant advocacy community of educators, scholars, and activists in New York City, I have often received requests to sign petitions to halt deportation proceedings of undocumented immigrants living in the US. I signed and at times received updates about a case, whether it had been overturned or whether it had failed and the individual was on the brink of deportation. Those who were deported seemed to just disappear; news of them or their families (if they returned together) was rare. As a former elementary school teacher and current professor who prepares teachers to work with multi-lingual learners, many of whom are immigrants or children of immigrants in New York City's public schools, I wondered what happened to the children: what are their lives like when they find themselves in a country they have only heard about, or a country where they only spent the first few years of their lives? How does this experience vary for students at different developmental levels? Certainly a 6-year-old's experience differs from that of a 16-year-old. On my sabbatical year, I went to Oaxaca, Mexico seeking answers to these questions. I chose Mexico because of its 1,900-mile shared border with the US and the high rates of people migrating between the two countries. I initially intended to conduct a study entitled *The Other Side of Deportation*, but I ended up focusing on families who were coerced to leave the US through governmental policies, or refused to be part of an oppressive and dehumanizing system. The families returned to Mexico due to the circumstances and challenges connected to being undocumented in the US, even if their children were US-born and therefore US citizens. Their stories highlight border crossings—especially among migrants who may lack documentation—are not consistently imposed upon people, but can also be a way they exhibit agency over their lives.

A few months after I arrived in Mexico to get the study under way I was introduced to Tim Porter, a photographer and journalist. Tim has spent eight years photographing children's shelters, families headed by single mothers, and street life in Oaxaca. As someone who has seen the power of multimodal approaches to research and its ability to more easily reach wider audiences—especially through my experience with documentary films—I was curious about the potential for making photography a part of this project. After discussing the focus of my work, Tim and I decided to collaborate and include black and white photography as another modality to share and humanize the experiences of transborder students and families. Tim followed three of the families in this study for six years in Mexico, and then, to a lesser extent, in the US. This book weaves together their words and photographs to contribute to a larger conversation about return migration, especially as it relates to education, language, and identity of young people.

Reference

Patel, L. (2015). Deservingness: Challenging coloniality in education and migration scholarship. *Association of Mexican American Educators Journal*, 9(3), 11–21.

PART I
Overview of Cyclical Migration

1

RETURN MIGRATION IN CONTEXT

Policies, Demographics, and Terminology

Yo soy de/I am from

Yo soy de aquí, pero también soy de allá
Yo vivo aquí y viví allá,
But is it possible to feel from two different places at the same time?
Soy del español y también del inglés,
I say "Hola" y también digo "Yes."
I am free, but before, I was caged,
The American dream? I found it somewhere else.
Yo soy del tercer mundo, donde se comen tacos
Yo soy del primer mundo, where mostly everyone uses an iPhone.
Yo soy Mexicana with some American roots
Yo soy de Mexico, but from the US too.
Yo soy de Oaxaca and this is where I want to be,
I was from Charleston, South Carolina, a place with good memories.
Ya no soy de mamá ni tampoco de papá,
I belong to myself now, it shouldn't be hard.
—Yauzin, a transborder college student

DOI: 10.4324/9780429340178-1

4 Overview of Cyclical Migration

FIGURE 1.1 Yauzin at Hierve el Agua, a natural springs and rock formation near the city of Oaxaca (2017).

Imagine a world where people are truly free. Free to move around to be with family and friends, free to work in the field they prepared for, and free to explore a world that has so much to offer and teach. This is a type of freedom that is available to some and denied to others by borders that limit their opportunities and determine the people and places they can access. Even in countries that purport to be free, only certain privileged individuals truly experience this freedom. For many, borders dictate their lives and serve as insurmountable hurdles in numerous aspects of their lives. A truly free world is one where borders are either inexistent or permeable, used to distinguish one politically administrative location from another, but not to mandate who belongs and benefits and who is left on the periphery.

This book is about young people and their families who cross physical and metaphorical borders. It features their words and their images. It highlights their joys, struggles, and experiences as dictated by their movements. It centers migrants, but is underpinned by larger national and transnational policies and structures that impact the everyday lives of people who migrate. These people have found themselves in a position where they have been coerced to return to their country of origin due to anti-immigrant policies or refuse to live in a nation that dehumanizes them. They often make this journey with their children, who are forced to start their lives anew in a country, culture, and language that may be largely unknown to them in many ways. These young people, to whom I refer as transborder (Stephen, 2007), are the focus of this book.

This chapter examines the global, transnational, and national contexts of Mexico and US that encourage or inhibit the movement of people. It begins with an overview of global migration and then delves into the historic and current policies that led to out-migration from Mexico and from the US. The next section provides an overview of the categories of return for mixed-status families who leave the US and the terminology used to describe them. Then there is a focus on the demographics related to return migration between the US and Mexico, especially among children and youth.[1] This chapter concludes with an overview of the sections and chapters of this book.

Global Movement of People Across Borders

Migration is a phenomenon that has touched nearly every part of the world. While movement ebbs and flows depending on various factors, people have always left the place they call home in search of a new or an additional home. What has changed is the increasing regulation and criminalization of these movements. When people are denied access to basic needs and freedoms, they are pushed to migrate in spite of external restrictions that allow this right to some and deny it to others. The process of leaving everything one knows, from country to culture to language, and venturing into the unknown is a difficult undertaking, to say the least. It is often emotionally draining, or worse yet, traumatizing, physically dangerous and tremendously costly for those who lack financial resources. It is not something one does for adventure; there are vacations for those yearnings (for those who can afford them). Instead, migration for many is an immense risk undertaken by those for whom it is not an option. The outcomes for migrants span the continuum of human experience, from people who lose life or limb in the process of crossing by land or dangerous waters to those who are able to build new lives and thrive in a new land. Yet in spite of the uncertainties migrants face, globalizing forces and international conflicts force people to put everything on the line to try to improve their circumstances, those of their families who accompany them on their journeys, as well as those who remain in the country of origin.

The movement of people is often categorized as "voluntary and involuntary, internal and international, authorized and unauthorized, and environmental, as well as victims of human trafficking," but migration has evolved in ways that go beyond current political frameworks (Suárez-Orozco, 2019, p. 1). As of 2017 there were 258 million international migrants globally, which accounts for 3.4% of the world's population and an increase of nearly 50% from 2000 (UN Department of Economic and Social Affairs, 2017). Children made up 20 million of the forcibly displaced international global migrants in 2016, and 8 million more that were displaced internally (UNICEF, 2017).

Increases in global migration are connected to growing levels of poverty, persecution, environmental disasters, war, and an overall inability to survive with dignity. Internal migration occurs within national borders when people are displaced from their homes. The most common movement is from rural towns to larger cities, especially in the case of those seeking employment. But for those who cross international borders, an additional and often difficult hurdle is obtaining permission to migrate by way of a visa. A person may qualify for a visa if they have close family members already living in the country (who are documented), possess certain credentials or skills deemed necessary, or are part of a quota that is granted to people from a given country, to name a few categories of admission. Others who experience persecution as outlined by the United National Human Rights Commission (UNHCR) are granted refugee status. They first move to a host or transit country and then, if the system works as intended, they are resettled in their final destination. However, less than 1% of refugees are approved for resettlement (UNHCR, 2019).

When people are unable to receive permission by way of a visa or refugee status to enter a nation, they migrate without authorization via land, water, or air. There are between 30–40 million undocumented immigrants globally, with at least one-third residing in the US. Those who cross international borders without authorization undergo numerous obstacles from the moment they set foot into the country: they risk being placed in detention or separated from family members and possibly sent back to live under the conditions they were trying to escape. Some undocumented immigrants apply for asylum status, petitioning a court to determine if they have a valid fear of being persecuted if they return to their country of origin. If their request is denied—as is more often the case—they are required to return. These differences in how people cross borders is a powerful reminder that the right to migrate is an unequal one.

In spite of the hopes and dreams that many migrants hold in moving to a new land, they do not always find their expectations met; worse, these dreams may turn into nightmares. As a result, migration can shift from a linear path to a cyclical process. And it is often national and transnational policies—or the absence of them—that push people to leave one country and enter another, and then return. This phenomenon continues to happen between different countries across the globe and is one that has always existed between the US and Mexico, neighboring nations with contentious histories that push and pull people to traverse their borders in their quest to live dignified and fulfilling lives.

National and Transnational Mexican and US Policies

> The US–Mexican border es una herida abierta [is an open wound] … Borders are set up to define places that are safe and unsafe, to distinguish *us* from *them* … A borderland is a vague and undetermined place created by emotional residue of an unnatural boundary. It is in a constant state of transition.
>
> *—Anzaldúa, 2012, p. 25*

The countries we call Mexico and the United States are not neutrally created and delineated territories. They are both first and foremost colonized land that was stolen from Indigenous peoples. It's estimated that colonizers eradicated 56 million of the 60 million Indigenous peoples who inhabited the Americas (Koch et al., 2019). Those who survived not only had their land stripped from them, but were also forced to abandon their traditions and languages. However, they fought for the rights to live on their own terms, and many Indigenous peoples and communities continue to do so across the Americas.

Although both countries have similarities in their histories, their trajectories have diverted significantly. The border between the US and Mexico is one example of how members of each nation have been and continue to be dis/empowered. This border has not only been contentious, it has been made and remade on multiple occasions, each time with land being removed from Mexico. In 1845 Texas became a part of the US after gaining independence from Mexico. However, Mexico did not allow Texas to secede, leading to the Mexican–US War.[2] The war concluded with the US exerting its power and the signing of the Treaty of Guadalupe-Hidalgo. The US paid Mexico $15 million dollars for half of its territory, which now make-up seven southwestern US states. At that time 80,000–100,000 Mexicans lived on this land, and had to choose between retaining their Mexican citizenship or becoming US citizens; being a citizen of both nations was not an option at that time (Henderson, 2011). The treaty also led to the now infamous border wall at its signing on February 2, 1848. Anzaldúa refers to this moment in history as a time when "The Gringo, locked into fiction of white superiority, seized complete political power, stripping Indians and Mexicans of their land while their feet were still rooted in it" (Anzaldúa, 2012, p. 29).

Cyclical Migration

The border has not only separated territories, but also separated certain people from crossing from one side to the other. However, migrants have been moving between Mexico and the US since the inception of the border, finding ways to circumvent its physical and political intentions, to keep certain people in place. Cyclical migration was part of seasonal agricultural work that drove migrations to the US, while family responsibilities brought them back to Mexico. This led to migratory patterns where people regularly traversed the border without authorization. While physically grueling, the political risks of such travels were relatively low. That change, however, in the mid-1990s tightened US border policies and restrictions and "'caged in' undocumented migrants fearful of returning to their home countries because of the risks and costs of reentry" (Roberts et al., 2017, p. 4). The increased border enforcement and patrol have made traditional cyclical migration patterns much more difficult. The changes in border policies led to drastic shifts in migration. For example, in the 1970s the majority of Mexicans in the US had moved back and forth between the two countries over a five-year period, whereas 30 years later the majority were staying in place without leaving the US due to the militarization of the border (Masferrer & Roberts, 2012). Another shift has been the labor sectors that draw Mexican migrants

8 Overview of Cyclical Migration

to the US. Initially, the jobs were primarily agricultural, and as a result, more seasonal. However, over time, Mexicans came to work more in the service sector, which tends to be year-round work that limits people's opportunities to leave the US.

Policies Promoting Out-migration from Mexico

> For Mexico, emigration has historically been a safety valve to economic pressures and political dissent that expose the repeated failure of the Mexican governments to generate equal opportunities for economic and social development.
>
> *—Délano Alonso, 2018, p. 44*
>
> For many mexicanos del otro lado, the choice is to stay in Mexico and starve or to move north and live.
>
> *—Anzaldúa, 2012, p. 32*

Mexicans have typically been pushed to migrate due to poverty, which is often an outcome of transnational policies. The Bracero Program was a form of temporary migration for Mexican men who were needed for US agricultural jobs that became vacant during the Second World War, when 10 million people in the US enlisted in the armed services. The program, in existence from 1942–1964, brought 4.5 million Mexicans to work in the US with governmental authorization. Workers outearned typical Mexican wages by up to ten times and were able to send part of their earnings as remittances to support family members in Mexico. However, these funds did not positively impact the Mexican economy over the long-term (Henderson, 2011). Furthermore, many workers endured deplorable conditions in the US. They earned subpar wages, lived in inhumane housing, and sometimes were abused by employers (Henderson, 2011). The end of the program led to an increase in Mexican undocumented immigrants as people remained in the US to continue agricultural work (Passel et al., 2012). Essentially, this was a circular migration program that led to the largest influx of immigrants entering the country in US history (Massey et al., 1987). It is also an example of how the US manipulated migrant labor from Mexico on its terms to benefit from it when needed and dispose of it when the need lessened. According to Gonzalez (1972), "When everything is added up, it turns out the Bracero Program took more than it gave" (p. 243).

Two decades following the end of the Bracero Program brought another wave of migration to the US. This influx was connected to increasing international debt of Mexico in the 1980s that led millions of Mexicans to suffer from a lack of access to nutrition, education, healthcare, running water, and electricity. Many Mexicans could not meet their basic needs nor provide opportunities for their children. As a result, undocumented immigration to the US reached all-time highs.

In 1994, Canada, Mexico, and the US signed the North American Free Trade Agreement (NAFTA), known in Mexico as Trato de Libre Comercio (TLC). This neoliberal reform assumed that each country would be an equal trading partner. However, Mexico started from a different, more disadvantageous place economically and subsequently experienced a different outcome. NAFTA set out to eliminate tariffs and other barriers to free trade among the three countries. It was touted as a reform that would bring Mexico out of poverty, while reducing the number of Mexicans who migrated to the US. In reality, NAFTA destabilized the Mexican economy. The removal of tariffs on corn imports from the US and Canada led small-scale Mexican farmers to abandon their subsistence farming, thereby losing their livelihoods. Mexicans then had to rely on imported food and basic goods at prices they could not afford. Additionally, when "rural subsistence possibilities disappear and when cities cannot absorb rural surplus, international migration becomes the only option for the whole family" (Roberts et al, 2017, p. 7). As a whole NAFTA benefited the US and Canadian economies, but it only minimally benefited the northern Mexican states while being especially detrimental to the southern states. NAFTA ultimately displaced 4.9 million farmers and led to record numbers of out-migration, leading Mexico into a severe depression (Fernández-Kelly & Massey, 2007).

Policies Promoting Out-migration from the US

The US is often touted as a nation where "The American Dream" becomes a reality. That may be so for some immigrants with documentation, those with formal education and its credentials, and those who come from wealthy backgrounds. These groups are best positioned to fulfill their goals and dreams in the country. Moreover, white immigrants benefit from racial privileges, while immigrants of color are confronted with white supremacy and xenophobia, two powerful and prevalent forces in the US. Immigrants lacking documentation are forced to the periphery of the country even as they struggle to defend their rights and their humanity.

While issues of immigration enforcement are prominent in national debates, this concept of limiting the movement of people was created after colonizers stole the land from Indigenous peoples and falsely claimed ownership and belonging. The construction of legal and illegal immigration began in the US in the 1880s "to placate economic and racial anxieties" of the white settlers (Little, 2019). They felt laborers from China were bringing down wages, which led to the Chinese Exclusion Act of 1882, the first federal law limiting immigrants. The rise of nationalism following the First World War (1914–1918) led countries to issue passports to regulate international border crossings. The criminalization of unauthorized border crossings began in the US in 1929 and has intensified since then. What has continued to shape immigration policies between the US and Mexico is the contradictory reality of the availability of jobs in the US, the lack of economic opportunity for laborers in Mexico, and the growing enforcement and militarization of the shared border.

Immigration is the purview of the US federal government; it is the sole entity that determines who can and who cannot enter the country and become a citizen. Comprehensive immigration reform generally includes a pathway to regularization for undocumented immigrants combined with enforcement measures. The last comprehensive immigration reform was the Immigration Reform and Control Act (IRCA), adopted during the Reagan administration in 1986 (Rosenblum & Brick, 2011). Under IRCA, 2.3 million of the 3 million people who applied to change their status and become legal permanent residents were Mexicans (Durand et al., 1999). IRCA had a dual purpose: to regularize the status of undocumented immigrants in the US prior to 1981 and to tighten enforcement by increasing funding for the US Border Patrol and heightening sanctions for employers who hired undocumented workers. Since then, the divisions and ideological differences between the two dominant US political parties (sometimes within them), have blocked any presidential or congressional effort to enact any comprehensive immigration reform. At the root of this debate is deservingness, which Patel (2015) explains is "a centuries-old frame to delineate humanness and worth ... deployed differently relative to different people in a settler society, formed on violent seizure and occupation of land" (p. 11). Over time the state has "debated, policy-ed and policed [deservingness] through governmentality, networked for the larger project of maintaining colonial sets of relationships" (Patel, 2015, p. 15).

Policies of deservingness continued during the Clinton administration with the 1996 enactment of the Illegal Immigration Reform and Immigration Responsibility Act (IIRIA). The one-sided, non-comprehensive policy that focused narrowly on enforcement made it easier to deport undocumented immigrants and increased the use of detention for individuals with pending deportation cases. The law opened the door to large-scale removals of mostly Mexican and Central American migrants, tripling deportation numbers in just three years (Rodriguez & Hagan, 2004). It also began an era that normalized the mass deportations that continue to the present day. IIRIA also imposed a 10-year ban for deported or returned undocumented individuals to apply to return to the US. It went even further and punished unauthorized re-entry as a crime that leads to a prison sentence.

Absent comprehensive immigration reform, piecemeal attempts emerged at the federal level to impact a subgroup of the undocumented population. The Development, Relief, Education for Alien Minors Act, or the DREAM Act, was an effort to allow young people who entered the US as minors to be placed on a path toward citizenship. The rationale that brought together Democratic and Republican politicians was that it was not the decision of the children to migrate to the US.[3] The DREAM Act was initially proposed in 2001 and lingered in the congressional labyrinth for more than a decade. The closest it came to being enacted was when the House of Representatives approved the bill in 2010, but the Senate defeated it by five votes. The bill—which has the potential to impact an estimated 1.4 million young people

(Heimlich, 2012)—was reintroduced in 2021 by a bipartisan pair of senators under the Biden administration exactly 20 years after its initial introduction. Time will tell if this act will become a reality or if it will remain another lowlight in the quest to open a pathway for a segment of the country's undocumented residents to more fully integrate into the US.

The 9/11 attacks in 2001, which destroyed the World Trade Center in New York and killed thousands of people there, in Pennsylvania and in Washington DC at the Pentagon, altered the country's perspective on immigration. Immigrants were no longer viewed as individuals fleeing difficult or dangerous situations to improve their lives and contribute to their new society, but rather as suspicious symbols of the terrorists who incited and carried out the 9/11 attacks.[4] This tragedy led to another tightening of immigration with the creation of a new arm of the Department of Homeland Security: Immigration and Control Enforcement (ICE). The agency was created in 2003 as the direct result of the conflation of immigration and criminalization, or "crimmigration" (Stumpf, 2006). ICE was charged with identifying undocumented immigrants to place into deportation proceedings. Depending on the administration, the role of ICE has vacillated from a focus on undocumented immigrants who have committed higher level federal offenses[5] to treating anyone in the US without authorization as a potential target for removal, as was the case under the Trump administration. ICE has wreaked havoc on undocumented immigrants and their mixed-status families through deportations, separations, and the cultivation of an overall sense of fear and surveillance (Capps et al., 2007; Hing, 2017).

While the federal government has been at a near standstill on immigration reform for decades, states have been more active in moving forward policies in favor of immigrants and against them. States cannot make decisions around immigration status, but their policies can impact the lives of undocumented immigrants. These localized reactions to the federal inaction are either meant to show immigrants without papers that they are welcome in a given context or to demonstrate to them that they are viewed as a threat who needs to be removed. The latter is especially the case in states that have had recent spikes in immigrant populations, and where the majority of the population is overwhelmingly White, English speaking, and threatened by the changing racial and linguistic landscape of their communities (Walker & Leitner, 2011).

Arizona is an example of a state where numerous anti-immigration sanctions have made the lives of undocumented immigrants even harder and more precarious. Arizona Senate Bill 1070, which was enacted in 2010, is referred to as the "show-me-your-papers" law. It essentially makes it illegal to be in the state without papers and has led to racial profiling. Slightly less than half of the states in the US require use of the E-Verify program, which makes it more difficult for people without Social Security numbers to obtain employment. The overwhelming majority of states bar undocumented immigrants from obtaining driver's licenses, making their lives exponentially more difficult because only the largest US cities have high-functioning public transportation systems. Some states have also made access to public higher education difficult for undocumented students by requiring them to pay the out-of-state tuition rates, which can be up to three times the rate of in-state tuition. States such as Georgia and South Carolina bar undocumented students from attending public universities, leaving private colleges as a last and unaffordable resort. These policies create hurdles that make the lives of undocumented people so difficult that leaving the US for their country of origin becomes a consideration as they seek to regain a sense of freedom and humanity.

Categories of Return

The impetus to migrate has been typically described as either voluntary or involuntary. However, this binary does not reflect the complexity of the current context and is especially problematic when applied to the migration experiences of people who live with a precarious status (Espindola & Jacobo-Suárez, 2018; Medina & Menjívar, 2015). To provide more nuance to the myriad reasons families return to their country of origin, I have created a continuum that lays out four categories that range from the most externally imposed to completely internal motivations to return (Figure 1.2).

Deportation   Coercion/Refusal   Free Will

FIGURE 1.2 Categories of Return Migration for Undocumented and Mixed-Status Families

The most commonly discussed form of return migration is deportation, or the forcible removal of individuals from a country by direct governmental action. Undocumented immigrants in the US are deported after they are detained by ICE in large-scale raids or with individual warrants. Also, depending on where they live, local or state police may refer their cases to immigration courts. People can be deported regardless of whether they are found guilty of the original reason for which they were detained by police, such as a traffic violation. Others are deported shortly after they are caught and detained after crossing into the US at a border. Some people are sent back immediately via expedited removal if they have only been in the US for a short time, while others go through immigration proceedings that can drag on for years due to the backlog in the court system. Both the number and the nationality of people deported are closely tracked. Deportation accounts for one-third of return migration to Mexico (Roberts, 2017).

The return migration category that follows deportation is coercion, which can also go hand-in-hand with refusal. Coercion stems from the consequences of anti-immigrant polices that oppress undocumented immigrants, and disproportionally impact people of color. It ranges from denying healthcare, higher education, driver's licenses to undocumented immigrants to creating a militarized anti-immigration atmosphere that causes people to live constantly under a state of fear and surveillance. It also affects individuals held in immigration detention centers awaiting trials who opt for "voluntary departure," in which they agree to immediately return to their country of origin on their own to shorten the time-frame or ban to return. This route is often taken to escape the trauma of living in detention centers that comes with improper nutrition, lack of medication and an absence of mental health care (Brané, 2007), as well as an increased risk of catching COVID-19 during the global pandemic. These forces coerce people into a corner. Denied of their basic rights by dehumanizing conditions, they can no longer sustain themselves. As a result of such coercion, and the realization that there are no other options, return becomes inevitable.

Refusal shares the same root causes as coercion, but it is a stance and conscious decision to remove oneself from oppressive forces. While an immigrant may have preferred to live in the country to which they migrated, they refuse to do so when they are stripped of their humanity and freedoms. Their return is a rejection of the policies and actions that suppress undocumented immigrants. It is an exertion of their agency, a declaration to live on their own terms. Refusal goes against the #heretostay movement and refutes the trope that their capacity to lead fulfilling lives is linked to any one country. Coercion and refusal are less visible and less monitored because they are not directly dictated by govern-mental agencies like deportations. However, they are both a reality for many families, and are the categories of return for the families whose stories are shared in this book.

The final category of return is free will, or a choice that is made in the absence of external forces and policies. It is a personal decision based on one's desires for the future. This could be someone who came to a country in order to make money and then eventually retire to their country of origin in order to be among family and friends. A return by free will may have been the original plan of many people who migrated to a new country, but only becomes a reality for some. It is the category in which the fewest people who have returned after being undo-cumented find themselves. In many cases, fully parsing out whether one is returning completely free of policies and external forces may never be possible.

These four categories go beyond the voluntary and involuntary binary to highlight the complexities of cyclical migration. But just like most frameworks, these categories are straightforward in theory, while the reality is much messier and interconnected. The return migration experiences of some may fit into more than one of these categories while others may have reasons that fall outside of this framework. But continuing to develop these categories is important to better understand the interplay of migration with personal autonomy and governmental forces in the lives of people who cross borders.

Terminology

Like categories, terms can also be limiting, but they provide descriptions that extend beyond the individual and delineate shared characteristics of a group. The category of immigrant includes the full range of people who traverse international borders. However, this term is too broad to adequately describe the particular experiences of the students who are the focus of this book: those who were born in Mexico or the US, lived in the US for a significant part of their childhood, and then returned to Mexico or were brought there for the first time. The literature uses a variety of terms to describe these students who are part of families with these kinds of cyclical migration histories.

One of the more common terms for children and youth who have lived and learned between the US and Mexico is "transnational" (Despagne & Jacobo Suárez, 2016; Zúñiga et al., 2008; Zúñiga & Hamann, 2009). It describes this population's experiences through its movements within, across, and beyond nations. "Binational" is another term used to refer to this group (Gándara, 2016), which also centers the nations and passage between two countries. Along those lines, "American-Mexican" further delineated students' nationalities and the directionality of their migratory experiences for those born in the US, as a reminder that the US is also a sending country and not only a receiving one (Jensen & Jacobo-Suárez, 2019; Zúñiga & Hamann, 2015). To broaden the scope of young people's movements, "international migrant children" has also been used "to raise the thesis that thinking of these students as 'Mexican' or 'America' is intrinsically incomplete … [and] ignores the realities of their pluri-national lives" (Hamann & Zúñiga, 2021, p. 105).

"Return migrant," also known as returnees or retornados, captures the dynamic and cyclical nature of migration (Cassarino, 2004; Jensen et al., 2017). It also touches upon the experience of "reconnecting to a social base, including a symbolic environment, that helps nurture and sustain one's sense of self, beyond satisfying instrumental, economic needs" (Roberts et al., 2017, pp. 20–21). Cruz-Manjarrez and Baquedano-López (2020) use the term "new returnee" to refer to people who were born in the US, lived in Mexico for three or more years, and return to the US, essentially completing a full cycle. Return migrant falls short as an overarching term here because it leaves out the experiences of children who do not share a country of birth with a parent and are not returning but are actually going to live there for the first time. (However, some of those children did become "new returnees" when they went back to the US.) But for the family unit that is back in their country of origin, return migration as a concept is fitting and representative of the reality of "return diaspora" (Espindola & Jacobo-Suárez, 2018, p. 60).

I have selected to use the term "transborder students" as it not only addresses the geo-political borders that delineate countries, but it is also inclusive of additional and equally significant borders that children and families navigate. It allows for attention to the ways language, culture, and school systems create borders that students traverse in their migrations (Stephen, 2007). "Transfronterizo children"

(Nuñez & Urrieta, 2020) has a similar connotation, while it directly acknowledges students' multilingualism, as well as the de facto national languages of Mexico and the US respectively. This term has been used to describe students who cross the Mexico-US border on a regular basis, to go to school or work in one nation while residing in the other (Relaño Pastor, 2007; Zentella, 2013).

All the terms outlined here serve to describe the focal students of this book in some ways, but are limiting in others. They all highlight different aspects of their mobile lives that can serve different purposes depending on the focus. Although I use the term "transborder students" throughout, I recognize that all of these terms can be useful in connoting various dynamics experienced by the young people featured in this book.

Mexico–US–Mexico Cyclical Migration Demographics

Although the US is commonly referred to as "a nation built by immigrants," this type of statement invisibilizes "Native Americans whose land was stolen in the creation of this country, as well as the descendants of enslaved people who were brought to this land against their will" (Carvajal, n.d.). However, globalization has pushed people to migrate to the extent that immigrants make up 13.7% of the overall US population (Budiman et al., 2020). There are also 37.1 million children born to immigrants in the country, who make up another 12% of the population. Taken together, they account for one-quarter of the US population as first- and second-generation immigrants (Waters, 2019). Mexicans are the largest immigrant group in the US at 28%, due to the history and proximity of the two countries (Budiman et al., 2020). There were approximately 11 million undocumented immigrants in the US in 2015, and of those about 50% were Mexican (Krogstad et al., 2017). Furthermore, half of Mexican-born children in the country are undocumented (Passel, 2011).

Migration is not linear. It is a cyclical and complex process, especially for children and youth. In 2010—the year when many of the families in this study returned to Mexico—1.3 million Mexicans in the US made their way back to Mexico, in part because of the reverberations of The Great Recession (2007–2009). This equates to almost 10% of the Mexican-born population in the US leaving the country (Masferrer & Roberts, 2012). These figures illustrate how the US-Mexico net migration rate balanced out at net zero for the first time in half a century (Passel et al., 2012).

The numbers of transborder minors who migrated from the US to Mexico quadrupled between 1970 to 1990 and has continued to grow (Zúñiga & Giorguli, 2019). It is estimated there are 800,000 transborder students with US schooling experiences in educación básica (preschool to 9th grade) in Mexico (Hamann et al., 2020). The US-born subgroup attending Mexican schools is estimated at 600,000, making them 3% of the overall student body (Jacobo-Suárez, 2017). When college-aged students are included, the figure rises to 700,000 (Jensen et al., 2017). Yet these numbers would be even higher if they included Mexican-born students who lived or attended schools in the US (these figures are not readily available). There are also hundreds of thousands of students in Mexico with a parent who resides in the US (Jensen et al., 2017). Overall, there are approximately two million young people who have lived between the US and Mexico; they are "the students we share" (Gándara & Jensen, 2021). It is these students and their families, who are (back) in Mexico, who are the focus of this book.

Book Overview

There are three sections in this book. Part I provides a framework to address concepts related to cyclical migration and introduces the transborder students and families in this study. Part II addresses the roles of identity, language, and education as they arise for students whose lives are structured by crossing borders. Part III describes lessons embedded in these students' stories, and offers recommendations for local, national, and transnational policy and pedagogy.

Part I includes two chapters that introduce the students, families, and communities where this research took place. Chapter 2, "Transborder Students and Families," describes the three communities where the students live or study. It provides an overview of the nine students from three different levels: (1) elementary school students, who were born in the US to undocumented parents and moved to Mexico for the first time; (2) secondary students who were born in Mexico and spent at least a decade of their childhood in the US and as pre-teens returned to Mexico; (3) and college students, who unlike the minors, made their own decisions to return to Mexico in the hopes of finding educational opportunities and freedoms they lacked in the US.

Chapter 3, "Family Return to Mexico," delves into the six reasons that drove the families in this study to leave the US for Mexico. While deportation is frequently thought of as the impetus of return, it was not a factor for these families. They came back for one or more of the following reasons, many of which were connected to living with a precarious status in the US: family unification (amid separation); financial hardships and gendered wages; lack of access to long-term health care; discrimination and exclusion; limited higher education access; and religious traditions and community obligations.

Part II builds from the internal to the external, beginning with who the students are (their identities), and moving out to their language practices, and then onto how they bring those aspects of themselves into schools. Each chapter addresses the topics across borders and countries and then compares students' experiences across elementary, secondary, and tertiary levels. Chapter 4, "Shifting National Identities and Immigration Statuses," examines the powerful role of national policies in the lived experiences of undocumented immigrants, as well as how family dynamics impact and create tensions in the continually developing identities of students. It delves into their own sense of self, which often differs from external perceptions, and labels that are imposed upon them by individuals and government entities.

There is also an overview of the complexities around dual nationality and mixed statuses among family members in the US and Mexico.

Chapter 5, "Language Learning, Unlearning, and Relearning," explores the rich and varied repertoires of students as they navigate complex linguistic landscapes shaped by family, community, schooling, economic necessity, and power. It explores the positionality of languages and their speakers across countries and how students experience a mixture of pride and shame when it comes to speaking Zapotec, an Indigenous language, as well as Spanish and English. It also explores how schools reify larger linguistic hierarchies without fully addressing the needs of multilingual transborder students.

Chapter 6, "Two Countries, One Education," focuses on one constant for students who migrate across borders: schooling. It provides a comparison between school systems in the US and Mexico. Then it shares the perspectives of primarily US-educated students who struggle with Spanish-medium instruction in Mexican schools, as well as different expectations around learning, behavioral norms, and historical understandings. It also includes the experiences of their educators, who feel unprepared to teach to the strengths and challenges of transborder students. Finally, this chapter addresses the difficulties of accessing higher education and the positionality of transborder students in English education programs.

Part III concludes with lessons that can be enacted within and beyond the two countries featured in this book. Chapter 7, "Policy and Pedagogy Implications," extrapolates from the stories and experiences of the nine transborder children and youth along with their families and educators. It considers broader implications for changes to policies and practices that center humanity, rather than artificial borders or demeaning labels. There are recommendations for national, binational, and transnational policies that could help make migration—in either direction—a choice one can make freely, as well as suggestions for pedagogical approaches that create a more seamless and relevant education for students whose lives and communities cannot be contained by the problematic conceptualization of national borders.

Finally, the Epilogue, "Where Are They Now?," provides a brief update on the current situations of most of the students in this study. It shares the direction their lives have taken seven years after the initial data collection. It highlights the successes and struggles students have faced, as well as how some have continued to move between Mexico and the US, as well as navigate metaphorical borders in their adolescence and young adulthood.

Notes

1 I refer to youth as young people in their teens and twenties.
2 Although this conflict is more commonly referred to as the Mexican–American War, I will refer to it instead as the Mexican–US War, because Mexico (and Canada) are part of North America and the Americas more broadly. Similarly, throughout this book I will refrain from referring to the US as America, and will not refer to people in the US as American except when quoting others.

18 Overview of Cyclical Migration

3 Undocumented youth have pushed back against the criminalization of their parents for bringing them to the US. They have insisted that their parents made difficult and courageous decisions to migrate due to the love they had for their children. They have labeled their parents as the "original Dreamers" (Ceja Garcia, 2017).
4 It is worth noting that the people implicated in the 9/11 attacks were authorized to be in the US.
5 Anyone found guilty of a crime in the US—regardless of immigration status—must serve the sentence handed down to them. Undocumented immigrants who are then put into deportation proceedings are essentially being punished twice for their offense.

References

Anzaldúa, G. (2012). *Borderlands/La frontera: The new mestiza* (4th ed.). aunt lute.

Brané, M. (2007). Locking up family values in the US. *Forced Migration Review*, 28, 39–40.

Budiman, A., Tamir, C., Mora, L., & Noe-Bustamante, N. (2020, August 20). Facts on US immigrants, 2018: Statistical portrait of the foreign-born population in the United States. Pew Research Center. www.pewresearch.org/hispanic/2020/08/20/facts-on-u-s-immigrants.

Capps, R., Castaneda, R. M., Chaudry, A., & Santos, R. (2007). *Paying the price: The impact of immigration raids on America's children*. The National Council of La Raza.

Carvajal, C. N. (n.d.). CUNY-IIE vision. www.cuny-iie.org/about.

Cassarino, J. P. (2004). Theorising return migration: The conceptual approach to return migrants revisited. *International Journal on Multicultural Societies (IJMS)*, 6(2), 253–279.

Ceja Garcia, I. (2017, September 17). We are NOT the original dreamers. https://m edium.com/@IvanCejatv/we-are-not-the-original-dreamers-6353374cc269.

Cruz-Manjarrez, A., & Baquedano-López, P. (2020). Los nuevos retornados de la migración maya yucateca en Estados Unidos. *Estudios fronterizos*, 21(4), e054.

Délano Alonso, A. (2018). *From here and there: Diaspora policies, integration and social rights beyond borders*. Oxford University Press.

Despagne, C., & Jacobo Suárez, M. (2016). Desafíos actuales de la escuela monolítica mexicana: el caso de los alumnos migrantes transnacionales. *Sinéctica*, 47, 1–17.

Durand, J., Massey, D. S., & Parrado, E. A. (1999). The new era of Mexican migration to the United States. *The Journal of American History*, 86(2), 518–536.

Espindola, J., & Jacobo-Suárez, M. (2018). The ethics of return migration and education: Transnational duties in migratory processes. *Journal of Global Ethics*, 14(1), 54–70.

Fernández-Kelly, P., & Massey, D.S. (2007). Borders for whom? The role of NAFTA in Mexico-US migration. *The Annals of the American Academy of Political and Social Science*, 610(1), 98–118.

Gándara, P. (2016). Policy report: The students we share. *Mexican Studies* 32(2): 357–378. doi:10.1525/mex.2016.32.2.357.

Gándara P., & Jensen. B. (Eds.). (2021). *The students we share: Preparing US and Mexican teachers for our transnational future*. SUNY Press.

Gonzalez, L. (1972). *San José de Garcia: Mexican village in transition*. University of Texas Press.

Hamann E., & Zúñiga V. (2021). What educators in Mexico and in the US need to know and acknowledge to attend to the educational needs of transnational students. In P. Gándara & B. Jensen (Eds.), *The students we share: Preparing US and Mexican teachers for our transnational future* (pp. 99–117). SUNY Press.

Hamann, T., Zúñiga, V., & López López, Y. A. (2020). Why the trauma, identity, and language (TIDAL) framework applies in Baja, California. AERA 2020, online.

Heimlich, R. (2012, July 9). Latinos overwhelmingly support DREAM Act. Pew Research Center. www.pewresearch.org/fact-tank/2012/07/09/latinos-overwhelmingly-support-dream-act.

Henderson, T. J. (2011). *Beyond borders: A history of Mexican migration to the United States* (Vol. 13). John Wiley & Sons.

Hing, B. O. (2017). Entering the Trump ice age: Contextualizing the new immigration enforcement regime. *Tex. A&M L. Rev.*, 5, 253.

Jacobo-Suárez, M. (2017). De regreso a "casa" y sin apostilla: Estudiantes mexicoamericanos en México. *Sinéctica*, 48, 1–18.

Jensen, B., & Jacobo-Suárez, M. (2019). Integrating American-Mexican students in Mexican classrooms. *Kappa Delta Pi Record*, 55(1), 36–41.

Jensen, B., Mejía-Arauz, R., & Aguilar Zepeda, R. (2017). Equitable teaching for returnee children in Mexico. *Sinéctica*, 48, 1–20.

Koch, A., Brieley, C., Maslin, M., & Lewis, S. (2019, January 31). European colonization of the Americas killed 10 percent of world population and caused global cooling. *The World*. www.pri.org/stories/2019-01-31/european-colonization-americas-killed-10-percent-world-population-and-caused.

Krogstad, J. M., Passel, J. S., & Cohn, D. (2017). *Facts about illegal immigration in the US*. Pew Research Center.

Little, B. (2019, July 2). The birth of "illegal" immigration: For a long time, it wasn't possible to immigrate "illegally" to the US. *History*. www.history.com/news/the-birth-of-illegal-immigration.

Masferrer, C., & Roberts, B. R. (2012). Going back home? Changing demography and geography of Mexican return migration. *Population Research and Policy Review*, 31(4), 465–496.

Massey, D. S., Alarcón, R., Durand, J., & González, H. (1987). *Return to Aztlan: The social process of international migration from western Mexico*. University of California Press.

Medina, D., & Menjívar, C. (2015). The context of return migration: Challenges of mixed-status families in Mexico's schools. *Ethnic and Racial Studies*, 38(12), 2123–2139.

Nuñez, I., & Urrieta, L. (2020). Transfronterizo children's literacies of surveillance and the cultural production of border crossing identities on the US–Mexico border. *Anthropology & Education Quarterly*. doi:10.1111/aeq.12360.

Passel, J. S. (2011). Flujos migratorios México-Estados Unidos de 1990 a 2010: Un análisis preliminar basado en las fuentes de información estadounidenses. *Coyuntura Demográfica*, 15–20.

Passel, J. S., D'Vera Cohn, G. B. A., Gonzalez-Barrera, A., & Center, P. H. (2012). *Net migration from Mexico falls to zero—and perhaps less*. Pew Hispanic Center.

Patel, L. (2015). Deservingness: Challenging coloniality in education and migration scholarship. *Association of Mexican American Educators Journal*, 9(3).

Relaño Pastor, A. M. (2007). On border identities: Transfronterizo students in San Diego. *Diskurs Kindheits- Und Jugendforschung*, 2(3), 263–277.

Roberts, B. (2017). Migration imes and ethnic identity: Mexican migration to the US over three generations. In B. Roberts, C. Menjívar & N. P. Rodríguez (Eds.), *Deportation and return in a border-restricted world: Experiences in Mexico, El Salvador, Guatemala, and Honduras*. Springer International Publishing.

Roberts, B., Menjívar, C., & Rodríguez, N. P. (2017). *Deportation and return in a border-restricted world: Experiences in Mexico, El Salvador, Guatemala, and Honduras*. Springer International Publishing.

Rodriguez, N., & Hagan, J. M. (2004). Fractured families and communities: Effects of immigration reform in Texas, Mexico, and El Salvador. *Latino Studies*, 2(3), 328–351.

Rosenblum, M. R., & Brick, K. (2011). *US immigration policy and Mexican/Central American migration flows*. Migration Policy Institute.

Stephen, L. (2007). *Transborder lives: Indigenous Oaxacans in Mexico, California and Oregon*. Duke University Press.

Stumpf, J. (2006). The crimmigration crisis: Immigrants, crime, and sovereign power. *American University Law Review*, 56(2) 367–419.

Suárez-Orozco, M. (Ed.). (2019). *Humanitarianism and mass migration: Confronting the world crisis*. University of California Press.

UN Department of Economic and Social Affairs (2017). International migration report 2017: Highlights. www.un.org/development/desa/publications/international-migration-report-2017.html.

UNHCR. (2019) Resettlement. www.unhcr.org/pages/4a16b1676.html.

UNICEF (2017). A child is a child: Protecting children on the move from violence, abuse and exploitation. www.unicef.org/publications/index_95956.html.

Walker, K. E., & Leitner, H. (2011). The variegated landscape of local immigration policies in the United States. *Urban Geography*, 32(2), 156–178.

Waters, M. C. (2019). Children of immigrants in the United States: Barriers and paths to integration and well-being. In M. Suárez-Orozco (Ed.), *Humanitarianism and mass migration: Confronting the world crisis* (pp. 308–324). University of California Press.

Zentella, A. C. (2013). Bilinguals and borders! California's transfronteriz@s and competing constructions of bilingualism. *International journal of the Linguistic Association of the Southwest*, 32(2), 17–50.

Zúñiga, V., & Giorguli, S. (2019). *Niñas y niños en la migración de Estados Unidos a México: La generación 0.5*. El Colegio de México.

Zúñiga, V., & Hamann, E. T. (2009). Sojourners in Mexico with US school experience: A new taxonomy for transnational students. *Comparative Education Review*, 53(3), 329–353.

Zúñiga, V., & Hamann, E. T. (2015). Going to a home you have never been to: The return migration of Mexican and American-Mexican children. *Children's Geographies*, 13(6), 643–655.

Zúñiga, V., Hamann, E. T., & Sánchez García, J. (2008). *Alumnos transnacionales: Las escuelas mexicanas frente a la globalización*. Secretaria de Educación Publica.

2
TRANSBORDER STUDENTS AND FAMILIES

FIGURE 2.1 Axianeydt and her grandfather, Miguel, stand at attention during the playing of Mexico's national anthem at the 6th grade graduation ceremony of Axianeydt's sister, Karla (2018).

DOI: 10.4324/9780429340178-3

> I am with my grandfather, saluting the flag. It reminds me of Mexico and all the experiences I had there. Being together with my grandparents made me happy.
>
> —*Axianeydt*

While return migration is a global phenomenon and happens across and within continents, this study looks at the movement of people between Mexico and the US. Mexicans make up the largest immigrant group in the US (Camarota, 2012) and comprise slightly less than half of the undocumented population in the nation (Passel & Cohen, 2019). The number of Mexican-origin people[1] living in the US and returning to Mexico was steadily increasing and eventually outpaced the numbers of Mexicans coming into the US between 2009 and 2014 (Gonzalez-Barrera, 2015). This study zooms into the experiences of nine transborder and their families, to move beyond statistics to stories.

This chapter begins with a framing of the methodological approaches and ways that photography became a central aspect of the study. It then introduces the three communities where the transborder students lived and/or studied and explains how I was granted access into these spaces, as this was my first time in Oaxaca. Then there is an introduction to each of the students and their parent(s) that outlines their migratory experiences from Mexico to the US and then back to Mexico.

Methodology Overview

This study was conducted to understand the experiences of transborder children and youth and the policies that drastically impact their lives. Too often, discussions of transborder students invoke numbers and labels and fail to focus on people's experiences. The study explored the realities of these young people by focusing on two overarching research questions and three sub-questions:

- How do US-born or raised children and youth in Mexico adapt to their border crossing experiences?

  - How do their national and ethnic identities evolve?
  - How are their language practices impacted?
  - How do they experience schooling?

- How do the experiences of elementary, secondary, and tertiary transborder students compare across levels?

A range of qualitative methods were used to gain a holistic understanding of the students' lives, which also included their parents, siblings, grandparents, and educators. The study consisted of interviews, artifacts, observations, and photography that came together in words, artwork, poetry, and images to tell—and also show—the varied and nuanced stories of living across borders.

- *Interviews.* I conducted interviews with 26 people in Mexico and one person in the US to learn the experiences of transborder students between the two countries. I interviewed each of the nine transborder students, one or both of their parents, and one of their teachers for the elementary and secondary students and a college professor for each tertiary student. Some of the elementary and secondary students and families were also included in the *Una Vida, Dos Países: Children and Youth (Back) in Mexico* documentary (Kleyn, Perez, & Vásquez, 2016). Their participation in the video meant they were interviewed a second time, which allowed for a continuation of their views and experiences. In order to contextualize larger (return) migration issues, I interviewed officials at the Instituto Oaxaqueño de Atención al Migrante (IOAM), the President of Ciénaga de Zimatlán where the elementary students were living, and the person who worked in the town's office to support families with US-born children with US passport applications. The interviews were conducted in English, Spanish, or bilingually depending on each person's preferences, that likely considered my own linguistic repertoire, race, and nationality (among other factors) as the researcher. Most of the interviews with the secondary and tertiary students, the college professors, and the IOAM administrator were primarily in English, while the interviews with the elementary students, their teachers, and community officials were primarily in Spanish.
- *Student Artifacts.* Each of the students were asked to create a product that encapsulated their border-crossing experiences. The younger students made drawings while the older students wrote poetry and created models. These artifacts allowed the students to communicate through a greater range of modalities that gave them more freedom of expression (Bagnoli, 2009).
- *Observations.* In order to get a better sense of students' school lives I conducted one classroom observation for the secondary and tertiary students. For high school students, I observed their English classes, and for college students, I observed a class on pedagogy and the English language. The administration at the elementary school did not permit me to enter classrooms during instructional time. But I was able to attend the graduation of one of the students the following year and to spend time on school grounds before and after the school day.

Research is never conducted in a vacuum. Issues of power between and within nations, societies, and people always come into play, and this study is no different. While researchers cannot eliminate such power imbalances, they can be transparent about their existence (Luttrell, 2000). Although I also come from an immigrant background, my whiteness has largely defined my experiences in the US and in Mexico as a researcher. In Oaxaca, for instance, I was granted access to different communities with relative ease. At one point, after asking an administrator if I could work with their school, I was told, "Por supuesto, tienes ojos claros" (Of course, you have light eyes). There were moments, though, when my skin color was perceived as a danger and a symbol of white supremacy. Once, when being introduced as a researcher to a family who had returned from the US, I was asked, "¿Eres de la migra?" (Are you from ICE?). As a US citizen racialized as white, I represented a system of power and violence to this mother. Although she was back in Mexico with her three US-born children, the father of her children remained in the US without papers, and her fear for his fate may have mediated our interaction. There were many more moments, some obvious and others that were surely invisible to me, that influenced this work and how people responded to me during the six months of data collection, the subsequent analysis, and the write-up of this study that are important to contextualize within these identities and power structures.

Photography Approach

The initial conception of this study did not include photography. However, about a month after I arrived in Oaxaca I was introduced to Tim Porter, a photographer who had been capturing the lives of children, families, and general street life in the region for a number of years. The idea for a collaboration emerged as a way to make the study more multimodal. We deliberated as to whether the photographs would serve to "'illustrate' or 'complement' the text, or ... 'speak' for themselves" (Luttrell & Chalfen, 2010, p. 198). The result turned out to be both, depending on the image and how or where it is included in the book. And because the photography continued five years beyond the interviews, artifacts, and observations, the photographs also served to extend the stories beyond the six-months of the other data collected during that period to allow for a longitudinal trajectory.

Tim photographed one focal family in the elementary, secondary, and tertiary group, respectively. The black and white photographs were taken over a six-year period from 2014–2020 to capture the lives of the families over that time in ways that words could not fully capture. The images had the power to "'speak back' to dominant or stereotypical images ... [and] redirect, contest and unlock the gaze" (Lutrell, 2010, p. 224). They were primarily taken in Oaxaca, Mexico, with some made in New York City prior to the COVID-19 travel restrictions.

We used the photo-elicitation method to attain additional insights into the photographs and transborder experiences that did not come across in the interviews and/or artifacts (Clark-Ibanez, 2004). We showed the photographs to the transborder students and families and asked them to (1) select several favorites that represented their experiences between Mexico and the US, and (2) reflect on what the images meant to them. We specifically asked them to recall the moment shown in the photograph and to consider how the images reflected their identity, at the time and presently. Those reflections are delineated with boxes around them under the relevant image, so as to differentiate them from quotes from the traditional interviews. Additionally, we included photographs that were not commented upon in order to connect and extend the concepts within the chapters. We gave the families the opportunity to exclude any photographs they did not wish to publish.

The Setting and Contexts

The study took place in the southern Mexican state of Oaxaca. The state—the fifth largest of Mexico's 32 states—has a population of 3,976,297 people (INEGI, 2015). Oaxaca is mountainous and has a Pacific coast whose beaches attract Mexicans and international tourists alike. Culturally, the state is known for its artesania, with many communities that work in textiles, clay, wood, paper, and other materials. Oaxaca's cuisine, especially its moles, has made it a gastronomic center of Mexico. It is a region known for its celebrations and festivals, the most prominent of which is the Guelaguetza, featuring the unique dances and traditional dress of each region of the state every July. The state's Día de los Muertos or Day of the Dead festivities gained more public attention with the release of the animated film *Coco*, which is partially based in Oaxaca.

FIGURE 2.2 The Cathedral of Our Lady of the Assumption in the central plaza—the zócalo—of Oaxaca.

26 Overview of Cyclical Migration

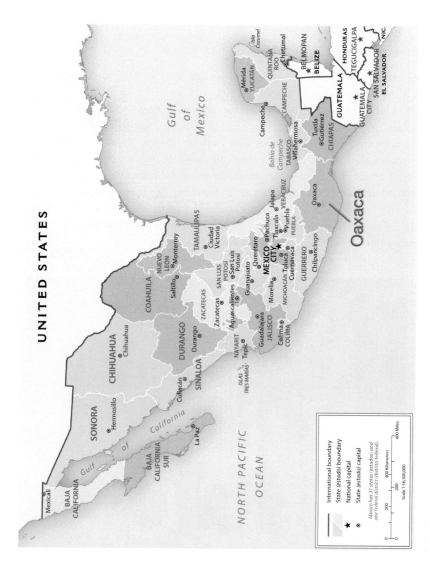

FIGURE 2.3 Map of Mexico.

Oaxaca is a hub for people from a range of backgrounds coming and going, by choice and by force, and for survival and pleasure. Although Oaxaca is more than 1,600 miles from the US border, it has one of the highest rates of migration to the US—due in part to its large Indigenous population, which experiences oppression and elevated rates of poverty (Heath, 2016). Approximately 32.15% of Oaxacans have an Indigenous background and are speakers of Indigenous languages (INEGI, 2015). The state is rich in linguistic and cultural diversity, with 16 official languages and unique regional customs that range from micro-cuisines to clothing design to religious observations that affect migration push and pull factors. Oaxaca is also home to a community of Black Afro-Mexicans, who predominantly live on the southwestern coast and were only officially recognized by the government through the census in 2020. The city of Oaxaca, the state capital, has a sizable number of mostly white US and Canadian residents. Some live there full-time, and others are known as "snowbirds" because they escape the winter cold of their home countries. They are a privileged example of cyclical migration. The Mexican government typically does not closely surveil their papers if they overstay their six-month tourist visa, which they are automatically granted at their point of entry. They, too, are immigrants, or seasonal migrants, but are often referred to as exclusively as expats. This inequitable and often racialized distribution of surveillance is yet another way to create hierarchies among those who migrate to secure their survival—and are referred to as immigrants—as opposed to those who come and go freely by choice and are labeled expats.

This study took place with students, families, and educators from three different communities, all in different parts of Oaxaca. Below I will explain each community's characteristics, as well as how I identified and was granted access to each site for this research.

Ciénega de Zimatlán: Elementary Students

Because I was a Fulbright scholar in 2014, the US Embassy in Mexico was aware of my study and reached out to me to ask that I serve as a conduit for information related to US citizens in Oaxaca. They requested that I share information about passport applications with families of any US-born children I may come into contact with, and also that I report any abuses of these children if I see them.[2] I asked if they could connect me with any communities that may be good sites for this research. They introduced me to the Instituto Oaxaqueño de Atención al Migrante, the local government agency that provides support for a range of migration issues such as translation of documents, transportation costs for deported or repatriated Oaxacans, and custody issues or legal guardianship of minors. After I explained my focus to the agency, they suggested I go to Ciénega and introduced me to the town's municipal president. I later learned he had lived for many years in Poughkeepsie, New York, where I spent part of my childhood and where my mother still lives. As a transborder individual, my study interested him, and he introduced me to Elizabeth, whose work in the municipality's office included helping parents apply for or renew passports for US-born children. She connected me with families who had returned from the US.

Ciénega is a rural town located 30 minutes by car from the city of Oaxaca. The population was 2,785 as of the 2010 census and the community is surrounded by scenic mountains where farmers grow marigolds, geraniums, and roses (INAFED, 2010). Agriculture is the primary occupation of the town, and local farmers cultivate corn, beans, alfalfa, tomatoes, and roses. Many families also raise farm animals, producing milk and cheese to sell or to use for family consumption. The town includes some small stores, bars, and restaurants that are often attached to people's homes. Ciénega is a migration community, with more women and children residents than adult men. Houses are made of cement and brick, some are painted in bright colors, and the larger of them have substantial iron gates out front. As in most migration communities, some houses are extravagant in comparison to their neighbors, and also are vacant, evidence that their owners have built them with money made while living in the US.

FIGURE 2.4 The town of Ciénaga de Zimatlán is a farm community located in a valley south of the city of Oaxaca.

The town center has a church that seats about 200 people. It sits on a square where children play and where events such as community festivals and religious ceremonies are held. A long municipal building houses the offices of the

President, the Ministry of Education, and the Treasury. Across the street is a small playground and a building where older adults gather to do arts and crafts. Just outside of town there is a sports center with a soccer field and outdoor fitness equipment. The town has one elementary school, which operates in two shifts. The morning session is from 8:00 a.m. to 12:30 p.m. and includes a 30-minute recess, leaving approximately four hours of instructional time. There is also one secundaria (grades 7–9). The closest high school (grades 10–12) is located in a nearby larger town about 10 minutes away by vehicle. The teachers mostly come from outside the community. At the elementary school, where all the primary focal students attended, there was one teacher per grade with approximately 25–35 students in a class. The principal estimated that throughout the school there were 3–5 transborder students who had previously lived in the US per class.

Out-migration is a decades-long reality in Ciénega that began with the Bracero program in 1942 and then transitioned into mostly undocumented migration due to economic necessities Remittances,[3] or money sent from family members working abroad to those who remain in their home country, are a significant part of the local economy. Juárez (2014) estimated one quarter of families in Ciénaga receive an average monthly remittance of $134 USD. Ciénegüeros, as the townspeople are known, have generally emigrated to the east coast of the United States, with Poughkeepsie, New York, and Chicago, Illinois being common destinations. The president of Ciénaga explained how Poughkeepsie, located 90 minutes north of New York City, became known as "Little Oaxaca." He said that around 1980 three cousins who had emigrated from Oaxaca were working at a New York City restaurant when the owner decided to sell that location and open up a new diner in Poughkeepsie. The cousins accepted the owner's invitation to relocate with him, and the move served as the impetus of the Oaxaca-Poughkeepsie connection that is going strong to this day. This illustrates Tilly's (1990) claim that networks migrate, rather than people and these networks support one another in identifying housing and employment while maintaining strong bonds with family members in their country of origin.

Twenty percent of the Latinx population in Poughkeepsie are Mexican and it's likely a large number of those have Oaxacan roots (Cortés, 2016). Each August, the Oaxacan community there holds a Guelaguetza, similar to the annual dance festival held in July in Oaxaca. Although no definitive statistics exist, Oaxacans from Ciénega are a mix of people with and without documents. Those who have the ability to travel back and forth return to Ciénega for quinceañeras, baptisms, and weddings, celebrations that draw hundreds of people together and are the focus of community social life in this otherwise quiet town. Some people who do not have papers also return for other economic or family reasons, but they stay for longer periods or even indefinitely due to the difficulties of crossing the increasingly militarized Mexico–US border. It is those people who are the focus of this book, and specifically the elementary students who were born in the US and arrived in Oaxaca for the first time with their parent(s).

Tlacolula de Matamoros: High School Students

In my quest for a community and a school with secondary students, I turned to a Fulbright colleague from the US, Dr. Rafael Vasquéz, whose extended family lives in Tlacolula. He had already been conducting research in the local high school, focusing on students' Indigenous language practices and how they shape their identities. He introduced me to the school administrators and the English teacher. After several meetings with them, I had the opportunity to meet with 11 transborder students in the school. Three of them became the focus of this study.

Tlacolula is a vibrant, regional market town of nearly 20,000 people about 30 minutes from the city of Oaxaca. Many people identify as Indigenous, and they speak or are at least exposed to the Zapoteco del Valle language. Many women dress in the traditional attire of brightly colored huipiles (blouses), equally colorful plaid skirts, and hand-woven cotton rebozos (scarves), which they wrap around their heads for protection against the sun or around their bodies as a sling to carry an infant. The young people, by contrast, dress in high-top sneakers, fitted jeans, crop tops or T-Shirts with English slogans or US brands. The main road is lined with shops selling clothes, the famous pan de cazuela, and mezcal, the smoky liquor distilled from agave plants that has helped define Oaxaca as a tourist

FIGURE 2.5 The sprawling market in Tlacolula de Matamoros has hundreds of vendors who sell every imaginable product—from vegetables to clothes to construction tools to live chickens and turkeys. One popular section holds rows of barbecues where shoppers can grill strings of pork sausages or sheets of beef.

destination. The town square has a church and an area for taxis. As in most Oaxacan towns, political murals by local artists espousing themes of social resistance adorn the walls of buildings. Locally, Tlacolula is known for its weekly market, where hundreds of vendors sell everything from livestock to souvenirs to endless types of dried peppers, and where food stands tempt shoppers with spicy goat barbacoa, tacos with fresh aguas or chocolate atole to wash them down with. The market draws locals, tourists, and residents of the city of Oaxaca.

Tlacolula has 19 schools. There are fourteen primarias (grades 1–6), three secundarias (grades 7–9) and two preparatorias/bachilleratos (grades 10–12). The high school students in this study all attended CETis – Centro de Estudios Tecnológicos, Industrial y de Servicios where classes begin at 7:30 a.m. and end at 3:30 p.m. There are CETis preparatorias/high schools throughout the nation and six in the state of Oaxaca that specialize in developing technological expertise. The school offers pathways to credentials in Microsoft, computer programming, accounting, and human resources administration, in addition to the core content curriculum. Although high school became mandatory in Mexico as of 2012, students are still required to pay matriculation fees, which limits the number of students who make it to and through high school. In 2014 CETis 124 had about 356 students and nearly 15% spent some time living and/or studying in the US. The student body comes from Tlacolula and surrounding towns that do not have their own high schools. Some students from neighboring communities even rent a small apartment or room during the week and return to their hometowns on the weekend as the daily commute would be too long or difficult.

Migration is a common phenomenon in Tlacolula, but unlike Ciénega, people from the town tend to migrate to the west coast of the US, specifically around Los Angeles (LA). California has the largest number of Oaxacans living in the US and is sometimes referred to as Oaxacalifornia. It's not uncommon to see people walking around Tlacolula with jerseys from LA sports teams. Nearly everyone living in Tlacolula can name family members who live or have lived in the US. The transnational ties are most visible after US paydays when people line up outside of the Western Union at the entrance to Tlacolula where locals wait to receive remittances from family members abroad.

Universidad Autónoma Benito Juárez de Oaxaca: College Students

After learning I was assigned to Oaxaca, I reached out to former Fulbrighters who had been living and working in the city to learn about life there and think about setting up my study. After explaining my focus on transborder students to Stephanie Abraham, she suggested I reach out to Yauzin. She was an undergraduate student in the language education program at the local public university: Universidad Autónoma Benito Juárez de Oaxaca (UABJO). I arranged for a Skype call with Yauzin, who agreed to take part in the study and helped to connect me with other students who had been back from the US in her language education

32 Overview of Cyclical Migration

program. As a result, all three tertiary students were not only undergraduate students at the UABJO, but also studying to become English language teachers. Unlike the elementary and secondary students who live and go to school in the same communities, students from the UABJO live in different parts of Oaxaca and are brought together by the college.

Nearly 20,000 students attend the UABJO, the largest of any public university in the state. It is located on a tree-lined campus whose stand-alone buildings—each dedicated to a different field of study—are connected by weaving sidewalks that pass through cafes and outdoor spaces where students work and socialize. A large and iconic library sits at its main entrance; soccer fields and basketball courts dot the perimeter. The UABJO admits students into 16 programs, among them medicine, nursing, architecture, accounting, law, and language education. Admission is highly competitive; for example, the language education program accepts only about 30% of applicants. The application process includes a fee of $700 MXN ($35 USD) as well as a Spanish exam in literacy, math, and history. While some students who score in the top percentiles are offered admission, many students are able to matriculate via bribes or connections to university personnel.[4] This makes the exam more of a performative measure, rather than one that weighs heavily in admissions decisions. Tuition for the UABJO is $7,500 MXN ($350 USD) for the first year and then $1,500 MXN ($100 USD) for the remaining undergraduate years. Surrounding private universities charge significantly more and their admission standards are generally lower due to their for-profit nature.

The students at the UABJO come from the various regions of the state of Oaxaca, including those from Mixtec, Zapotec, and Chatino Indigenous communities, as well as students who have lived in the US. While US-based universities require liberal arts core classes, UABJO students primarily take classes in their area of study. Students develop strong connections to their majors through comparsas (parades) during Día de los Muertos, sports tournaments and special lectures with their peer group. The Facultad de Idiomas (Faculty of Languages) often referred to as Idiomas, in particular, has a disproportionate number of transborder students who have lived in the US and are able to leverage their English as a strength. However, the language program does not require English proficiency as an entrance requirement. Instead, they accept students of all levels so as not to privilege those who had language learning opportunities over those who did not. The English practices of admitted students, however, are evaluated and they are then assigned to leveled cohorts. Those in the beginner groups have the double task of learning English as they also learn the pedagogy to teach students new languages. Each incoming class in Idiomas has about 250 students, with 45–50 in each of the five leveled groups. By the second year, the groups are reduced to about 35 students due to attrition.

The UABJO is known for its students' and faculty's political activism. There are frequent closings due to union matters and student led protests around larger social issues such as femicides. Art is one form of protest that permeates Oaxaca and the UABJO is no different. At the time of this study in 2014 there was a powerful mural on the outside wall depicting the 43 students from the all-male teachers' college Escuela Normal Rural de Ayotzinapa who disappeared and were thought to have been murdered by corrupt police officers or drug dealers in the state of Guerrero. There were numerous protests throughout the country and calls for the government to admit their role in this tragedy, which has yet to be solved.

Meeting the Students and Their Families

The book will focus on nine students from three different levels: (1) elementary school students born in the US to undocumented parents, who due to their dual nationality have the option to return to their place of birth; (2) secondary students born in Mexico who spent more than a decade of their childhood in the US, and as pre-teens/teens struggle to fit in with their peers and acclimate to Mexican schools; and (3) college students, who unlike the minors, had some agency in the decisions to return in the hopes of finding educational opportunities and freedoms they lacked in the US. Five identify as female and the other four identify as male. Each student has three to six years of living in Mexico, either for their first time or after spending most or at least half of their childhood in the US. This time frame allows them to have a longitudinal view of their initial arrival to Mexico and their transition into different aspects of their lives between the two countries over time.

TABLE 2.1 Student information.

Level	Student	Age at Time of Data Collection**	US-born or Age Arrived in US	Age of Arrival/ Return to Mexico	Years (Back) in Mexico
Elementary	Axianeydt	10	US-born	6	4
	Karla	8	US-born	4	4
	Melany	7	US-born	4	3
Secondary	Sharely	16	1	13	3
	Brayan	16	3	12	4
	Melchor	17	1	13	3
Tertiary	Yauzin	23	9	17	6
	Ricardo*	22	5	18	4
	Erik	22	11	18	4

*I was not able to reach Ricardo or his parents prior to this book's publication, so their names are pseudonyms. All other study participants chose to use their real names, to increase their visibility and share their stories openly.
**The interview and observations data were collected in 2014 and the photographs were taken between 2014 and 2020.

The elementary group included one sibling pair—Axianeydt and Karla—whose brother Zayd was too young to take part in the interview and artifacts, and perhaps more so because of his unbounded energy and inability to sit still for long. But he appears in numerous photographs throughout the book. The other students all had brothers and sisters, but they did not actively participate in the study. Two of the secondary students had US-born siblings, creating a mixed-status dynamic in their family and one of the tertiary students had a sibling who remained in the US and is a recipient of the Deferred Action for Childhood Arrivals (DACA) program.

Elementary Students

Many transborder students at the elementary level are born in the US and arrive in Mexico with the privileges afforded by US citizenship; as of 1998, they also have the ability to obtain dual nationality through a Mexican-born parent. Depending on their age of arrival in Mexico, these elementary students may have limited memories from their time in the US. They may only speak Spanish, and possibly an Indigenous language, if they had only little or no schooling during their time in the US.

Axianeydt, Karla, and their brother, Zayd, were born in Chicago, Illinois, to Mexican-born parents who were undocumented in the US. In the interviews, however, they made it clear they are a family with four children: two boys and

FIGURE 2.6 Alberta at the grave of her oldest child, Jezreel, in Ciénaga de Zimatlán. He died as a toddler in the United States. She did not see his grave until she herself returned to Mexico six years later (2015).

Transborder Students and Families   35

two girls. The first-born boy, Jezreel, died just 15 days after the second child, Axianeydt, was born. The cause of his death at just two months shy of his second birthday was never determined, but his place in the family is not forgotten. He is buried at the local cemetery in Ciénega where family members in Mexico can visit him throughout the year and where he is celebrated annually during Día de los Muertos.

> When I found out I was pregnant, I felt very happy and I emigrated to the US thinking I could get ahead there because I was a 21-year-old single mother. But when my son died, I could not return to Mexico because I was illegal and my daughter, Axianeydt, who was two weeks old, was in the custody of her father's aunt. I could not see my son buried. When I returned to my town in 2011, I found his grave marked with a cross, his name, and the dates of his birth and his death. Although many years have passed, I will always mourn his passing.
>
> —*Alberta*

Axianeydt, the oldest daughter, is followed by Karla, who is about one year younger and Zayd is the youngest brother. The three of them are like most siblings, closely bonded but also at times at battle with each other. The girls especially love to create art and Axianeydt has a special fascination with drawing animals and anime, inspired by Japanese animated media. She has filled numerous sketch pads with her drawings, and many of her pieces adorn the walls of the bedroom she shares with her mother and siblings in their grandparent's home in Ciénega.

Their mother, Alberta, left for the US at the age of 21 to work and to escape the judgment of her small town when she learned she was pregnant. She crossed through Mexico and the Rio Grande with her sister and niece. They first made it to California and then New York. There she eventually reunited with her children's father after her first son was born. They migrated numerous times within the US between New York, Illinois, and Virginia. Alberta primarily worked in restaurants as a hostess and learned the English that was needed to be successful in that position. The children's father also worked in restaurants and held every possible position so that he was eventually able to manage all aspects of day-to-day operations. He also made time in his very full schedule to work as a tattoo artist.

The final elementary student in this study is Melany, a seven-year-old girl with a slightly shy but friendly disposition. She was born in a suburban town about 45 minutes north of New York City. Although close to the largest US city, this town has open space and requires a car to get around as public transportation is limited. Melany's parents departed for the US at different times, but both crossed by land and water. Her father, Emanuel, paid $2,500 USD to a coyote, someone who acts as a guide or smuggler of migrants across the US border. Emanuel made various trips between the countries when crossing was less

FIGURE 2.7 Axianeydt, left, and Karla in their bedroom in Ciénaga de Zimatlán, Oaxaca (2018).

challenging than it has become. He has also spent more time in the US than his wife and children, having arrived a year prior to them and remained for two years following their return to Mexico. Emanuel's wife, Leidy, arrived in the US when she was pregnant with Melany, although she didn't know it at the time. Both are both glad that Melany and her younger sibling were born in the US so that they have the opportunities afforded by citizenship. Emanuel lived in New York State for a total of eight years while Leidy was there for a little more than five years with her US-born children.

The family has a small house with a spacious yard that looks onto the mountains surrounding Ciénega. With their savings from the US, they bought a building in town that they made into a restaurant with a few amusement park rides outside. The business has become more of a bar since local people are not in the habit of eating out, while going to socialize over drinks is commonplace.

Secondary Students

All the secondary transborder students featured in this book can only share their journey to the US through the stories they have been told by family members. They all left Mexico between the ages of one and three and returned about a decade later as pre/teens. Being 12 or 13 years old is generally a time of challenge and growth for most adolescents. Moving to what feels like a new country, enrolling in a new middle school, or secundaria, and studying in a different language at this time makes their experiences even more difficult. When I met the three students, they were already in high school. The principal arranged a meeting between myself and a group of students who had lived in the US so I could share my work and research plans with them. I ended up working closely with three of the students, who I collaborated with to form a club in their school they called "The New Dreamers." They read *Los Otros Dreamers* (Anderson & Solis, 2014) as a starting point to discuss their shared experiences crossing borders. They also contributed to the creation of a guide to educate teachers in Mexico about other transborder students who had been educated in the US.

My initial meeting with Brayan at his high school stands out. His English teacher told me he was very excited because he thought he was going to meet "Tatiana de los niños," a well-known Mexican singer whose songs are geared toward educating and entertaining children. I told him I was sorry, but I was "Tatyana de los adultos" and hoped he wasn't too disappointed. He seemed to get over it quickly and jumped into asking me a series of questions about traveling to the US and scholarship opportunities to study there. Of all the students in this study, Brayan seemed to be the most upset about being brought back to Mexico and the most set on returning to the US.

Brayan, 16, returned to Mexico at age 12 after living in the US for almost a decade. His parents crossed the border first when Brayan was a toddler, leaving him with his grandmother. They sent for him three months later. He was three years old when he crossed the border with a coyote. Their family first lived in Los Angeles, California, and then moved to Fort Myers, Florida. His mother picked oranges, babysat, and worked at McDonalds; his father worked in construction as a roofer. His parents eventually separated, but Brayan recalls how they "were always thinking about paying rent and bills, buy the foods and it was a lot of money and they were just working for that kind of thing." Brayan's younger brother, Cristopher, was born in California, making them a mixed-status family. The significant difference between the brothers is that Cristopher's dual nationality allows him to travel more easily between the US and Mexico, while Brayan cannot cross the Mexico–US border freely.

Melchor is a tall, lanky teenager with hair that usually incorporates some sort of styling product. He is often connected to his cell phone and has a laid-back way about him. Melchor, 17, isn't a big talker, but when he speaks it always with precision. He was born in an Indigenous mountain town where most residents speak Zapotec. His family migrated to the US in stages. First his father went, then before Melchor turned two he and his brother were brought across the border by posing as the sons of an unrelated woman. When his mother made it across a little later, they were reunited in California where they lived for 12 years. After returning to Mexico, Melchor's mother gave birth to a girl. The family lives between a smaller home in their Indigenous village and an unfinished brick house with breath-taking mountain views that is closer to high school in Tlacolula.

FIGURE 2.8 Sharely in her high school class in Tlacolula de Matamoros (2015).

Prior to returning to Mexico, Sharely could only remember a life in the US. But she tells the story of being brought to California by a woman who claimed her as her son as if she had a vivid memory of it. The plan nearly went awry when an airline worker invested in traditional gender norms asked why the baby "boy" was wearing earrings. The woman thought fast and said that in her culture it was common for boys to have earrings. Sharely made it to the US, earrings and all, to be reunited with her parents. Her father had been in the US since he was 12 in order to work and send money to his family in Mexico. He had been back and forth three times. Sharely's mother, Tere, is from the same small, country town as her father, but they didn't meet until they both lived in the US near Los Angeles. After meeting, they returned to Oaxaca where Sharely was born, then left for the US in stages, her father followed by the mother and then Sharely. The family grew to two children when Sharely's sister, Nancy, was born in Los Angeles. Their time on the West Coast involved numerous moves dictated by her parents' employment situations. As a result, Sharely changed schools multiple times throughout her elementary and middle school years. At the age of 13 Sharely experienced her second airplane ride, back to Mexico, this time with her own documentation as a girl. It was the first airplane she could remember. She said it felt like a roller coaster, an apt analogy for the ups and downs and twists and turns of the lives of transborder students.

FIGURE 2.9 Sharely, right, with her sister, Nancy, outside of their home in San Juan Guelavía, Oaxaca (2017).

Tertiary Students

The college students featured in this section spent the majority of their formative middle childhood and adolescent years in the US and made the decision to return to Mexico. They are the exception rather than the rule when it comes to educational attainment of young adults who are back in Mexico. All three students have made their way to college in Oaxaca and are studying to become English teachers (this choice is discussed in Chapter 6). Just as in the US, where most undocumented students are unable to go to college due to numerous structural obstacles that vary from state to state (Chavez et al., 2007; Nguyen & Serna, 2014), students who return to Mexico after growing up in the US also face difficulties entering higher education, even as Mexican citizens. However, for some transborder students a return to Mexico may be due to the focus on college readiness in US K-12 schools, which shapes their aspirations and makes Mexico the most viable option for higher education (Cortez Román & Hamann, 2014). Their struggles across countries have led them to become what Heidbrink calls "experts by experience" (2020, p. 66). Their in-depth understanding of the realities of being undocumented immigrants in the US, have led them to understand the impact of white supremacy, xenophobia, and dehumanizing anti-immigrant policies that require people to live under constant fear and surveillance.

It's worth noting that all three of these students returned to Mexico prior to the 2012 announcement of the Deferred Action for Childhood Arrivals (DACA) executive action signed by President Obama. Each would have likely qualified for this temporary status, as they were minors when they arrived in the US. Under DACA they would have been given a Social Security number for working purposes and a stay from deportation that would have been renewable every two years.[5] Additionally, DACA could have led to increased earning opportunities to support themselves and their families, access to driver's licenses and health insurance, and the ability to enroll in and more easily pay for college (Gonzales et al., 2018). DACA is only available to those living in the US, making it out of reach for transborder students who returned to Mexico. Erik, one college student featured in this study, shared his reaction to DACA after his friends in the US became recipients of the program: "I was like 'Damn, why didn't I stay?'" We don't know whether the availability of this program would have affected the choices of the transborder youth who decided to return to Mexico rather than to remain in the US.

FIGURE 2.10 Yauzin at the Universidad Autónoma Benito Juárez de Oaxaca (UABJO), where she earned a bachelor's degree in language education and currently teaches English to undergraduate students (2020).

Yauzin, the first tertiary student in this study, was nine when she crossed the Mexico–US border with her younger brother, Tony, and mother, Herminia. Her older brother, 15, decided to stay in Mexico. The three flew from Oaxaca to

Sonora and then passed what Yauzin referred to as "la famosa línea." Their crossing was a difficult one, because they were caught by US border patrol and held in a detention facility. "We spent over a week in a very small room where they kept like 20 people and we couldn't take a shower for like 10 days," Yauzin recalls, "so you can imagine how frustrated we were." They were finally transported by their coyote to Charleston, South Carolina, where her father, Antonio, had been living for a year and saving money to bring over his family. When she arrived, Yauzin says, she noticed that "the streets, they were nice, they weren't bumpy [like in Mexico] and they don't have much public transportation, buses or anything, everybody has a car." The family was living in a trailer home, which she initially saw as a "cool" house and car combination. Eventually, she came to a different conclusion about her living arrangements: "In the States I lived in a trailer home and here in Mexico I lived in a house [with my family growing up]. How crazy is this?"

Yauzin is fiercely independent and has strong convictions about what is right and wrong. She exhibited these characteristics as a child, and they were heightened by her transborder experiences. Once, for example, on her 17th birthday in South Carolina, Yauzin was in the car with her father, Antonio. She had her birthday cake on her lap when a police officer pulled them over. Antonio received a traffic ticket but then the officer learned it was Yauzin's birthday he let her father go instead of booking him, which would have risked his deportation. (However, her father was not permitted to drive home so Yauzin's uncle came to get them). Yauzin said she knew that not arresting her father was the right thing to do, that it would have been wrong to separate her, or any child, from their parent. In that moment, though, she also realized how precarious their lives were in the US. Yauzin started her education in the US in middle school as a 6th grader and experienced her first direct contact with Black people, who constituted most of the students and teachers in the school. She recalls just one white student and a few white teachers, and she was one of a small number of Latinx students. As one of the few students learning English as a new language, she was teased, but she started excelling in high school, even making it to honors and advanced placement (AP) courses.

Ricardo appears shy at first, but with the right questions he opens up, and when he does he has a lot to say. He was brought to the US at age five, the youngest of the tertiary students in the study. He and his younger sister had false documents when they traveled to be reunited with their parents in California, who had crossed three years earlier with a coyote. His crossing is a blurry memory, but what stands out to him is being in a cramped Tijuana hotel room in the Mexican border city with seven other people. Once he was reunited with his family in the US, he spent the remainder of his childhood attending elementary, middle, and high school in the country. He returned to Mexico with his family at age 18, just two months short of obtaining a high school diploma. While he was hoping to move right into college studies upon his arrival, he was discouraged but not dissuaded once his US transcripts were evaluated and it was determined he would need to complete the final semester of his bachillerato or high school. He registered in a high school and took the necessary classes to reach that final step in his K-12 education, and eventually graduated.

Beyond the disappointment of having to repeat some of his high school education, Ricardo says he felt mostly positive about returning to Mexico. He was eventually able to adapt to speaking Spanish with the help of his parents, but is still learning about cultural aspects of Oaxacan life that don't always translate from his US experiences. One aspect that stands out is living with continuous protests by the teachers' union and other public employees in response to the educational reform imposed by former President Enrique Peña Nieto in 2013. The controversial aspects of the reform included the cancelations of permanent teaching positions, the requirement of exams for new teachers to attain permanent positions, and evaluations of working public sector teachers to keep their positions. The protests block streets, close businesses such as gas stations, and shut down the university. Ricardo views his time in Mexico as a "good experience" that has helped him group up "personally, psychologically, and emotionally too."

Erik, 22, is fashion-forward with his trendy clothes and sneakers. He has many friends and centers his life around futbol, or soccer. He went to the US at age 11 with his mother and younger brother. During the border crossing in Arizona, they became separated and were detained by border patrol before reuniting. Erik remembers it as "an adventure," but his journey was not absent of fear, especially when he was separated from his sibling and mother. They made their way to California and finally New Jersey. His father had been in the US for six years, meaning Erik had lived nearly half his life without the physical presence of his father. He recalled that the reunion felt "strange," but overall he was happy to finally live with both parents. Erik's most vivid memory of the arrival to New Jersey was spending the first few days in shopping malls where he noticed how different the stores were from those in his hometown.

Erik enrolled in 6th grade, where he faced the oftentimes frustrating challenge of learning in English-only classes. "One time I cried because I had homework," he said, "and I didn't know what to do and I didn't have a lot of friends yet. I told my dad to put me in a plane and tell my aunt to go pick me up here in Mexico." He eventually made friends with Latinx peers who spoke Spanish and became accustomed to life in the US. He completed high school before returning to Mexico.

More than anything, what defines the lives of transborder students in the US and Mexico is continual change. They transit from one country to the next, shifting cultures and languages as they go, adapting to the complicated social and educational experiences of new schools, and all the while experiencing the arrival and departure of family members. It is a labyrinth of change, one they must negotiate again and again. The aim of this study is to show how this navigation happens across and within countries, how it occurs in the context of cyclical migration, and how it affects the lives, the learning, and the languaging of students and families.

Notes

1 I refer to Mexican-origin people as those either born in Mexico or born in the US to Mexican parents.
2 Although I did not see any abuse, it was noteworthy that the US government wanted to collect such information from me; it was unclear to what extent this was about surveillance as opposed to ensuring the protection of US citizens.
3 Remittances are the largest source of foreign income in Mexico. In 2016 Mexican immigrants in the US sent $27 billion USD to family members in the country (Harrup, 2017).
4 Admissions practices at the UABJO and other Mexican universities mirror those of US colleges that grant preferential entry to applicants with legacy claims, alumni connections, or family members who are generous donors.
5 In 2020 the fee to apply for DACA or to renew it every two years was $495 USD.

References

Anderson, J. & Solis, N. (2014). *Los otros dreamers*. Jill Anderson & Nin Solis.

Bagnoli, A. (2009). Beyond the standard interview: The use of graphic elicitation and arts-based methods. *Qualitative Research, 9*(5), 547–570.

Camarota, S. A. (2012). *Immigrants in the United States: A profile of America's foreign-born population*. Center for Immigration Studies.

Chavez, M., Soriano, M., & Oliverez, P. (2007). Undocumented students' access to college: The American dream denied. *Latino Studies, 5*, 254–263. doi:10.1057/palgrave.lst.8600255.

Clark-Ibanez, M. (2004). Framing the social world with photo-elicitation interviews. *The American Behavioral Scientist 47* (12) 1507–1527.

Cortés, Z. (2016, December 7). Little Oaxaca: How Mexican immigrants revived Poughkeepsie. *Voices of NY*. http://voicesofny.org/2016/12/little-oaxaca-how-mexican-imm igrants-revived-poughkeepsie.

Cortez Román, N. A., & Hamann, E. T. (2014). College dreams à la Mexicana … agency and strategy among American–Mexican transnational students. *Latino Studies, 12*(2), 237–258.

Gonzales, R. G., Ellis, B., Rendón-García, S. A., & Brant, K. (2018). (Un)authorized transitions: Illegality, DACA, and the life course. *Research in Human Development, 15*(3–4), 345–359.

Gonzalez-Barrera, A. (2015, November 19). More Mexicans leaving than coming to the U.S. Pew Research Center. www.pewresearch.org/hispanic/2015/11/19/more-mexica ns-leaving-than-coming-to-the-u-s.

Harrup, A. (2017, February 1). Remittances to Mexico hit record $27 billion in 2016. *Wall Street Journal*. www.wsj.com/articles/remittances-to-mexico-hit-record-27-billion-in-2016-1485978810

Heath, H. (2016, June 15). Mexico's Indigenous population continues to face high rates of poverty. Panoramas Scholarly Platform. www.panoramas.pitt.edu/health/mexicos-indi genous-population-continues-face-high-rates-poverty.

Heidbrink, L. (2020). *Migranthood: Youth in a new era of deportation*. Stanford University Press.

INAFED. (2010). Ciénega Zimatlán. Instituto Nacional para el Federalismo y el Desarrollo Municipal de Oaxaca. www.inafed.gob.mx/work/enciclopedia/EMM20oaxaca/m unicipios/20013a.html.

INEGI. (2015). Población y lengua indígena. Instituto Nacional de Estadística y Geografía . www.inegi.org.mx/temas/lengua.

Juárez, A.M.A. (2014). *Remesas colectivas y familiares: Los dividendos del capital social: Un estudio de dos comunidades mexicanas en contexto de migración internacional.* Universidad Autónoma Benito Juárez de Oaxaca, IISUABJO.

Kleyn. T., Perez, W. & Vásquez, R. (2016). Una Vida, Dos Países: Children and Youth (Back) in Mexico. [Documentary] www.unavidathefilm.com.

Luttrell, W. (2000). "Good enough" methods for ethnographic research. *Harvard Educational Review,* 70(4), 499–523.

Lutrell, W. (2010). "A camera is a big responsibility": A lens for analysing children's visual voices. *Visual Studies,* 25(3), 197–200.

Lutrell W., & Chalfen, R. (2010). Guest editors' introduction: Lifting up voices of participatory visual research. *Visual Studies,* 25(3), 197–200.

Nguyen, D. H., & Serna, G. R. (2014). Access or barrier? Tuition and fee legislation for undocumented students across the states. *The Clearing House: A Journal of Educational Strategies, Issues and Ideas,* 87(3), 124–129.

Passel, J. & Cohen, D. (2019, June 12). Mexicans decline to less than half the U.S. unauthorized immigrant population for the first time. Pew Research Center. www.pewresearch.org/fact-tank/2019/06/12/us-unauthorized-immigrant-population-2017/.

Tilly, C. (1990). Transplanted networks. In V. Yans-McLaughlin (Ed.), *Immigration reconsidered: History, sociology and policies.* Oxford University Press.

3
FAMILY RETURN TO MEXICO

FIGURE 3.1 Karla and her grandmother, Maria, in the garden of their home in Ciénaga de Zimatlán, Oaxaca (2018).

No inmigramos por gusto. [We do not immigrate because we want to.]
—*Alberta*

DOI: 10.4324/9780429340178-4

46 Overview of Cyclical Migration

Melany estaba llorando porque todo el tiempo es encierro en los Estados Unidos y aquí fue libertada. [Melany was crying because she was always locked up in the United States and here she was freed.]

—*Leidy*

The families in this study had to make multiple difficult decisions about migration that drastically impacted each person member and their future. Mexico's poverty and corruption drove them out as they could not meet their basic needs. In the United States, federal and state policies limited their ability to live freely and build a dignified life; these legalized ideologies of belonging and deservingness forced them to the periphery of society (Patel, 2015). The families returned to Mexico for a range of reasons, nearly all directly related to the hardships of living undocumented or as mixed-status families in the US. The reasons included:

- family unification (amid separation);
- financial hardships and gendered wages;
- lack of access to long-term health care;
- discrimination and exclusion;
- limited higher education access; and
- religious traditions and community obligations.

Although each family identified one problem in particular as their primary motivation for leaving the US, in most cases a combination of these circumstances forced their return.

Family Unification (amid Separation)

Family reunification is the primary reason immigrants living in the US return to Mexico (Krogstad, 2016). The irony is that as family members are (re) united on one side of the US-Mexican border, they are simultaneously separated from family members on the other side (Suárez-Orozco, 2015). They live in a constant state of uncertainty, not knowing when or if they will see some of their family again. When a family member dies, relatives who do not have documents to travel often cannot attend the funeral. To avoid this fate, some Mexicans in the US return. It used to be that migrants could return for short visits to be with family prior to the increased enforcement at the Mexico–US border and the heightened activity of ICE in the interior (Hazán, 2014). These continual border crossings have become more dangerous and costly, requiring those who reunite with loved ones to endure a more long-term and life changing return. Two families in this study identified reunification with parents/grandparents as a primary reason for their return.

FIGURE 3.2 Alberta with her children, Axianeydt, Zayd and Karla, on the day of their First Communion in Xochimilco, Oaxaca (2019).

Alberta's return reunited her with her aging but active parents after a decade-long separation. She wanted to spend quality time with them and enable her three US-born children—Axianeydt, Karla, and Zayd—to meet and get to know their grandparents. She and the children moved into her parents' three-bedroom house near an extended family of cousins, aunts and uncles. The grandfather is a farmer, and the children had the opportunity to ride horses, milk cows and experience the cycle of birth and death that occurs among farm animals. The children's move to Mexico simultaneously united them with their family in rural Ciénega, but separated them from their father, who stayed in New York City, where he worked and sent money for the children.

Family also pushed Sharely, her younger sister, and her parents to return to Mexico. She recalls:

> I found out we were coming back to Mexico because my dad started to miss his parents so I felt that I wanted to meet my grandparents too. I was excited to come here because I wanted to find out how my culture is because I hadn't been since I was a little girl. My mom wasn't really happy with the idea but now she's fine.

FIGURE 3.3 Axianeydt, left, in the corral of her grandparents' farm in Ciénaga de Zimatlán, Oaxaca, with her brother, Zayd, and a cousin (2015).

Sharely's dad, Alberto, also noted that he and Sharely agreed about returning. "Ella nos decía que nos regresáramos porque quería conocer a sus abuelitos ahora que están vivos" (She always told us to come back to Mexico because she wanted to meet her grandparents while they're still alive). Sharely's homecoming not only reunited her with her grandparents, but, like Alberta's children, gave her access to an extended family with a long history in a small, country town. Family alone, however, was not the only reason for their return. Alberto also says that it was "por la renta, que nos venía seguido y a veces no había trabajo. Mis niñas estaban desesperadas de estar todo el tiempo encerradas. De la escuela a la casa y de la casa a la escuela, era la rutina diaria" (for the continuing need to pay rent and sometimes there was no work. My girls were tired of being locked up all the time. From school to home and from home to school, that was the daily routine).

Family and economics are interconnected factors of return. Employment opportunities, or the lack of them, impact the quality of life one is able to provide for their family. Alberto's family would find themselves tied to their home and school for the girls when there was a lack of resources to do much more. Employment status and wages also factor into the extent to which migrants in the US can support their family members in Mexico by way of remittances (Hazán, 2014). Financial reasons, connected to a lack of freedom, were a through thread for nearly every family.

FIGURE 3.4 Sharely's grandparents, Margarita (third from left) and Alfredo (behind her), and other family elders bless the food at the wedding of Sharely's aunt (2015).

> My culture. I see that and it's my culture. I love it. I appreciate it. Maybe I was born in front of a bowl of mole, maybe that's why…. There's a real big canasta of bread. A lot of turkeys. The more the turkeys, the better the wedding (at this wedding there were two dozen). This is Mexico, the culture.—Sharely

Financial Hardships and Gendered Wages

> We started to do something before our life is gone. I was working all day every day, it's not a life. Working for 12–13 hours Monday to Thursday, Friday night, Saturday night, restaurant double job and I was feeling tired and all the money I make go away so I haven't seen nothing. I said, "Why am I working so hard and I don't have nothing?"
> —*Emanuel, Melany's father*

Emanuel and other undocumented immigrants in the US often feel like they are running on a hamster wheel: they work constantly but never get ahead financially. As a result, they have little time to spend with family or to enjoy their lives. The obvious irony of Emanuel's situation is that the family left Mexico for the US "por lo mismo cuestión de vida económica más que nada" (for the same reason of economics more than anything), as his wife, Leidy, explained.

50 Overview of Cyclical Migration

In addition to the freedoms described in the US Constitution, economic freedoms determine the quality and dignity of one's life. Emanuel said, "I didn't feel free, I didn't feel like I was a person." He and his wife lived in an economic hole they could not escape, no matter how much they worked. As undocumented immigrants they could not extricate themselves from the constraints of the US capitalist system that is set up to benefit corporations and the wealthy. Many immigrants are robbed of the life they envisioned in the US, and as Brayan's mother explains below, "return defeated."

For Emanuel, returning to Mexico has brought him a new sense of hope. "You've seen my house," he says. "It's little house, but no payments, no rent, no nothing. Plus, we try with the restaurant right now, hope so, we're going up and growing and growing and we feel happy, we feel free. It's all different, my way to think, you know, to feel happy right now." Leidy shares that sense of happiness that comes with that feeling of freedom. Being back, she says, allows her to enjoy "mi casa, estar con mi esposo, mi familia, más que nada sentirse libre" (my house, to be with my husband, my family and most of all to feel free).

The elementary school students like Melany didn't fully grasp why they were returning, but the high school students understood better their parents' challenges. Brayan provides the perspective of a child watching his parents struggle in the US. "You were not paid as much as you thought you were going to get paid," he says, "and you had to pay a lot of bills, rent and food." He also understood that being Mexican was a reason to underpay people and cause them to struggle more. Nonetheless, when Brayan was told at age 12 his family was returning to Mexico, he was not happy. His mother says:

> Él estaba muy enojado porque lo habíamos traído. Si se adaptó luego, pero si me reclamaba el lugar, el inglés, que él estaba mejor que vivía mejor allá. Siempre le he dicho que yo no lo puedo tener allá y un sueldo de una mujer no sirve para los hijos. Es muy caro y es muy poco el sueldo. Las familias regresan derrotadas.
>
> [He was very angry because we had brought him back. He adapted later, but he still complained to me about the place, the English, that he was better off there. I have always told him that I couldn't afford living there with him. A woman's salary is not enough to have children. Everything is expensive and the salary is very low. The families return defeated].
>
> —*Martha, Brayan's mother*

Martha separated from Brayan's father and had to support her sons on her own in Florida. Being a single mother is difficult under any circumstances, but in the US women make 82 cents to every dollar that white men make, and Latinas make 59 cents to every dollar white men make (Bleiweis, 2020). These studies do not factor in immigration status, meaning they do not take into account that employers often take advantage of undocumented immigrants by paying them less than their citizen counterparts (Borjas & Cassidy, 2019). The reality of being a single, undocumented, Latina mother made surviving in the US an even larger obstacle for Martha and played a significant factor in her family's return.

Limited mobility leads to a lack of economic opportunity. For example, Emanuel says there was immense "stress on my wife; she wanted to get a job, drive like everybody else." However, many states don't allow undocumented immigrants to have a driver's license, greatly impeding their ability to work and study. In most US cities and towns, car culture is the norm and public transportation is limited, increasing the burden on those who can't drive legally. "If we could have the papers and license and all this straight, it would be different," Emanuel says "All your brain and ideas, everything changes because you're comfortable." For many undocumented immigrants, however, such comfort is out of reach. Federal and state policies and laws enclose them in what Jong-Min refers to as an invisible prison with invisible bars (Kleyn, 2013).

Lack of Access to Long-Term Health Care

Less than half of Mexican-born immigrants residing in the US had health insurance in 2012 (Consejo Nacional de Población, 2013). The US Emergency Medical Treatment and Active Labor Act of 1986 requires most hospitals to treat anyone who shows up in their emergency room, regardless of immigration status or possession of health insurance. Only some states provide health insurance to undocumented immigrant minors and even fewer offer such insurance to adults (Edward, 2014). As a result, undocumented immigrants with chronic health issues that need long-term care may be forced to return to their country of origin to seek treatment.

Melchor's family faced this fate after his father, who worked as a lumberjack, was injured while scaling a tree:

> Me lastimé la espalda y así fue que ya no pude trabajar, pero afortunadamente mi esposa pudo seguir trabajando para mantener a la familia. Necesitaba ir al doctor para que me diera tratamiento porque me lastimé la columna y dos discos. Por eso decidimos regresar.
>
> [I injured my back at work, that's why I could not work, but fortunately my wife could continue working to support the family. I needed to go to the doctor in order to be treated because I injured my backbone and two discs. That's why we decided to come back.]
>
> —*Feliciano, Melchor's father*

In seeking treatment for his back injury, Feliciano faced two insurmountable challenges: the lack of money to pay out of pocket for the therapy and medication he needed and the necessity for his wife to be the sole financial provider of the family during his recovery. She, like Martha (Brayan's mother), made less as a female undocumented worker than her husband, and she couldn't earn enough to meet the family's daily needs. Feliciano's medical issue quickly became a family financial issue, one that eventually forced the family's return to Oaxaca.

Discrimination and Exclusion

> American people always discriminate you when they know you're Mexican. I think all kinds of people have to have the same opportunities. ... you are not better than anyone just being American citizen, they are not the owner of the country.
>
> —*Brayan*

Even though the secondary students only lived in the US through middle school, they understood clearly the hierarchies of citizenship in this country. These hierarchies emerged from a long and troubled history between the US and Mexico. The boundaries of the contemporary US includes tribal lands stolen by violence or fraud from Native Americans. Furthermore, seven US states were formed from territory that either partially or fully belonged to Mexico prior to the 1848 Treaty of Guadalupe Hidalgo. Brayan's words allude to these contentious aspects of US history, which highlight the nation's unethical acquisition of territory and delegitimization of entire groups of people.

Many of the students expressed similar sentiments. Yauzin said that during her childhood in South Carolina she learned firsthand that discrimination was commonplace:

> When I was a child [in Mexico], I did not even know how to make fun of someone else and when I got there [to the United States] I knew that even nationality was a good excuse to make fun of people. Mexican, beaner, wetback, the N-word, crackers, so for me that was like, "Oh my god, this is sad."

The parents also experienced rampant racism and being treated as stereotypes, social factors that affected their return. The families lived in a constant state of fear and trauma, subjected to degrading tropes about Mexicans committing crimes and stealing "American" jobs as they are also victims of a culture of hyper-policing that is regularly inflicted upon Black people (Rios, 2011). Sharely felt that, in the US, "you are not going to be happy because they are always going to be watching you." This reality pushes families to escape this surveillance and to seek out the opportunity to live and learn freely.

Limited Higher Education Access

> When I was in the beginning of high school, I told my parents, "After I finish high school, I'm moving back to Mexico because I want to keep studying and

here I'm not going to do that." They thought I was kidding. The last day of school I was like, "I need my plane ticket, I want to go." That's when they saw that I was serious.

—Yauzin

Yauzin always planned to continue on to college, and she was set on making it a reality. However, the state of South Carolina stood in her way. Its anti-immigrant policies are among the most restrictive in the nation (Reich & Barth, 2012). One law, House Bill 4400, bans undocumented immigrants from attending public universities and receiving public financial aid or scholarships for higher education. Had Yauzin stayed in the US after high school, she would have had to attend a private university in the state—often a prohibitively expensive choice—or move to another state that allowed undocumented students to enroll in public universities. However, this option would have brought about complicated and expensive residency and high school graduation requirements in order to avoid paying exorbitant out-of-state tuition fees.

Yauzin's mother talks about her daughter's dislike of the US, saying she told her, "Es que a mí no me gusta aquí. Yo estoy aquí porque ustedes me trajeron. Yo solo estoy aquí nada más hasta que yo estudié la high school, terminando la high school me voy" (It's that I don't like it here. I am here because you brought me. I am only here until I study in high school. When I finish high school, I am going). Yauzin's younger brother was a different story, perhaps because he came to the US at the age of six (instead of nine like his sister) and had fewer memories of Mexico. Yauzin's mom explains, "Ya con el otro niño fue diferente. Como él era chiquito le fascinó estar allá y vio diferente la situación a lo de ella" (With the other kid it was different. Since he was younger, he loved everything there and saw everything differently from her.)

Because Yauzin returned to Mexico without her parents, she initially lived with her older brother and then her aunts. Two years later her dad was deported after police stopped him while driving to work, allegedly for driving with his lights off, which Antonio disputes. Police asked him for documents, then immigration officials took him into custody and deported him. Yauzin's mother eventually decided to follow her daughter and husband in this reverse chain migration, leaving only her youngest child in the US with his aunt in California. South Carolina also bans undocumented immigrants from obtaining driver's licenses and supports collaborations between local law enforcement and ICE, both of which led to her father's deportation.

The story of the return of Yauzin and her family reflects the entire range of challenges undocumented immigrants face in the US: white supremacy, racism, and xenophobia, which are formalized in anti-immigrant policies and discriminatory treatment that coerce people out of the country.

FIGURE 3.5 Yauzin and her parents in their apartment in North Charleston, South Carolina (2005).

Religious Traditions and Community Obligations

Among the eight families in this study, only one returned to Mexico for a reason not directly connected to their immigration status in the US or anti-immigrant sentiments, policies, and actions. Erik's family returned to Mexico for a civic, religious, and Indigenous tradition known as the mayordomía. In Oaxaca, as in communities throughout Mexico and Central America, people of the village assume the role of mayordomo, or patron of the town. One community member in Stephen's study explained, "Mayordomos are helping take care of the gods, who in turn take care of us" (2007, p. 59). In that role, they are responsible for organizing and funding the annual celebration of the town's patron saint. It's common for Oaxacans living in the US to return for a mayordomía and fulfill their obligation to the town. Erik's father explains:

> Venimos por la promesa que teníamos con el patrón de aquí. Aquí nosotros fuimos los mayordomos, fuimos los encargados de hacer la fiesta, preparar la comida, hacer el baile, de juegos, de estar aquí. La fiesta dura como cuatro días porque hacen juegos de basquetbol, la fiesta patronal, la mayordomía, y esas cosas. Sí, porque nosotros tenemos que vestir la iglesia, comprar las reses para la comida de toda la gente. Casi todo lo de la fiesta lo pusimos nosotros porque uno se compromete y uno pone todo eso. Nosotros compramos las flores, los juegos artificiales para que se divierta la gente en la noche, pagamos la misa y damos una limosna. Yo pienso que unos 80 o 100 mil pesos se gasta uno. Nosotros lo prometimos y como somos católicos pues la cumplimos.
>
> [We came back for the promise we made to the patron saint of the town. Here we were the religious administrators. We were in charge of the celebration, preparing the food, organizing the dance, the games, being here in general. The party lasts around four days because there are basketball games,

FIGURE 3.6 Townspeople carry bouquets of flowers into the church during a fiesta patronal in San Sebastián Abasolo, Oaxaca.

the party, the management of everything, among other things. We also have to decorate the church, buy the cattle for the meal to feed all the people. We do almost all of the fiesta ourselves because you commit yourself and you do it. We buy the flowers (for the church), the fireworks so that people can enjoy themselves at night, we pay for the mass and we give alms. I think it cost $80,000 to $100,000 Mexican pesos. We promised it and since we are Catholics, we did it.]

The fiesta patronal is the town's annual celebration of its patron saint that generally takes place for up to a week and includes religious and social activities that culminate in the mayordomía. The mayordomos or the religious administrators ask the saint for something along the lines of health, financial stability, employment, or peace, in exchange for sponsoring the events. The traditions of the mayordomía changed as a result of migration. Prior to large scale migration to the US by way of the Bracero program there was less money to pay for elaborate celebrations, but increased participation from community members. In some Oaxacan communities mayordomías were eradicated or at risk of disappearing (Stephen, 2007). But with the help of money earned abroad, mayordomos often spend more than $4,500 USD to fulfill their obligations. The cost of being mayordomos partly pushed Erik's parents to live in the US, earn money for this honor and tradition, and then return.

Student Agency in Migration Across Levels

The Mexican-born students in this study were 1–11 years of age when they migrated to the US, often to reunite with one or both parents who had preceded them. Depending on their age, some children were told that they would be leaving their hometown for a new country, while others were taken across the border without any discussion. Yet in making these difficult decisions, "adults are actively engaged in the process of 'developing' their children toward the goals and values they hold for them" (Orellana et al., 2001, p. 587).

When the children traveled to Mexico—either for the first time or to return—their experience differed based on their age and the extent to which their families involved them in their deliberations and decisions. The elementary students were 3–6 years old when they were brought to Mexico for the first time. The country was an abstraction for them. Their conceptions of it were gleaned through photographs and virtual conversations with family members such as grandparents, aunts, uncles, and cousins they had never met in person. Alberta, the mother of three children born in the US (and a fourth who died), did not discuss her decision to return to Mexico with her children. Nor did Emanuel and Leidy talk about it with their daughter Melany, who was 4 when she was taken to Mexico. In both cases, the parents made a life-changing decision that affected their children in multiple ways and which they are only beginning to understand as they grow up.

The 12- to 13-year-old secondary students had very limited agency, or ability to make choices on their own behalf, when their parents told them they were returning to Mexico. But they did have different reactions to it as students who only had memories of living in the US and heard stories about their short-lived experiences in Mexico. Both Melchor and Brayan remember how the decision to leave was shared with them and their reactions:

> We finished dinner and I see that my parents are packing up, and I said, "What's going on?" They said, "We're going to tell you the truth, we are moving back to Mexico." I was really shocked I said, "Why? Can't we just move to another county or something? Because I don't want to go back to Mexico."
> —*Melchor*

> When my mom first told me that we were going back to Mexico, I was so sad I started crying. I didn't want to came back because I grew up there and I feel so bad because it was not my decision. It was theirs and I couldn't do anything … I didn't even heard the rest of the story she was telling because I was crying. I didn't want to come back. The next day in the morning she told me that she bought the tickets to come back.
> —*Brayan*

Both boys were initially quite upset and resistant, but after some time in Mexico they felt better about being there. After being back for four years, Brayan said he now "feels good" and "got used to it," although the initial return was difficult. Melchor, too, says the immediate shock has worn off. He was eager to one day return to the US to see "qué tal está la vida" (how is the life there) in order to compare living in the two countries.

While some students learned about their family's return quite suddenly, Sharely and her sister participated in ongoing family discussions about the possibility of returning to Mexico. Her parents were divided. Her mom leaned toward staying in the US, while her dad yearned to reunite with his parents. Sharely was curious about what life was like in her parents' hometown and wanted to get to know her grandparents and other family members. The family came to a consensus and left California, with Sharely looking forward to the move and to live a life free of the economic anxiety and fear of deportation that plagued the family in the US.

The college students were all at the cusp of young adulthood at 17–18 years of age when they returned to Oaxaca. They exercised different levels of agency in their family's decision to return to Mexico.

Ricardo's family began to plan their return after his father lost his job. Although Ricardo was 18 and legally an adult, his parents did not consult him. "It was more of a 'this is what we're doing' rather than a choice," he says. He wasn't resistant to this change, however, because he understood the challenges of living undocumented in the US. He initially thought that "this could be a new

FIGURE 3.7 Sharely's family—Alberto, left, Tere, Sharely and Nancy, her younger sister, and their dog, Chiquita (2015).

beginning … I can adapt. It'll be easier than here [in the US]." He saw it as a potential opportunity and understood that it would be difficult for them to stay in the US if his father was not working.

Erik knew well in advance that his parents were going to return to Mexico to fulfill their responsibilities as mayordomos in their community. His father returned first, and then his mother. Erik and his brother remained in the US while he finished his senior year classes and even took his final exams early in anticipation of leaving. In his final days in New Jersey, Erik's younger brother injured his leg playing in a soccer tournament and it fell on Erik, with the support of a church community and extended family, to care for him. When he made the last-minute decision to return with his brother, he said, "I was kind of happy 'cause I was going to meet my family again, but at the same time it was hard 'cause I was going to miss my graduation." He thought he would eventually return to the US and in the meantime attend soccer school in Mexico and play there professionally.

As mentioned earlier, Yauzin, unlike the rest of her family, was determined from her first day in South Carolina that her time there would be temporary. Her stance strengthened as she learned about the state's anti-immigrant policies, which worsened during her seven years there. Based on her experiences, she believed that "South Carolina is a very racist state." "I'm not going to say in general," she says, "but I found many racist people there." She demanded that her parents purchase a one-way flight for her to Mexico the day after her high school graduation, which they did, albeit begrudgingly.

After being back in Oaxaca for four years, Yauzin applied for and received a ten-year US tourist visa. This process was made easier because she had returned to Mexico as a minor at age 17. She may not have been able to do the same if she had left even one year later after she reached the age of 18. Any adult who has a record of being in the US without authorization must wait out a ban of up to 10 years before they can even apply to re-enter the country, as per the 1996 Illegal Immigration Reform and Immigration Responsibility Act (IIRIA). With a tourist visa in hand Yauzin has been able to visit her younger brother in California as well as friends and former teachers in South Carolina. She has also traveled to parts of the country that were new to her, such as New York City.

FIGURE 3.8 Yauzin in New York City, visiting on a tourist visa seven years after she left the United States and returned to Oaxaca (2016).

Clearly, the agency children have when it comes returning or moving to Mexico from the US varies greatly; some simply follow their parents' wishes, others participate in a broader family conversation, and a few come to independent conclusions about where to live. Not surprisingly, the oldest students had the most powerful say. The secondary students were most caught off guard with the reality of a return, although Sharely's experience demonstrates that students can be involved in a family dialogue that leads to consensus. Most of the elementary students were too young to form an opinion about migrating to Mexico. Their experience mirrored that of the secondary students who were brought to the US as toddlers or preschoolers, also not old enough to weigh in about their family's journey or understand the consequences of such a life-altering move.

Regardless of the level of agency students had in their migrations, their journeys across borders led these nine students to experience the challenges and potentials that relate to their sense of identity, heightened awareness about language amid growth and loss, and educational experiences that were uplifting in some aspects and limiting in others. The next section delves into each of these areas as they were lived by students, and reflected upon by their parents and educators.

References

Bleiweis, R. (2020, March 24). Quick facts about the gender wage gap. Center for American Progress. www.americanprogress.org/issues/women/reports/2020/03/24/482141/quick-facts-gender-wage-gap.

Borjas, G. J., & Cassidy, H. (2019). The wage penalty to undocumented immigration. *Labour Economics*, 61, 101757.

Consejo Nacional de Población. (2013). *Migration and health: Mexican immigrants in the U.S.* Secretaría de Gobernación/Consejo Nacional de Población.

Edward, J. (2014). Undocumented immigrants and access to health care: Making a case for policy reform. *Policy, Politics, & Nursing Practice*, 15(1–2), 5–14.

Hazán, M. (2014). Understanding return migration to Mexico: Towards a comprehensive policy for the reintegration of returning migrants. Center for Comparative Immigration Studies. https://ccis.ucsd.edu/_files/wp193.pdf.

Kleyn, T. (Producer & Director) (2013). Living Undocumented. [Documentary] www.Livingundocumented.com.

Krogstad, J. M. (2016, February 11). 5 facts about Mexico and immigration to the US. Pew Research Center. www.pewresearch.org/fact-tank/2016/02/11/mexico-and-immigration-to-us/.

Orellana, M. F., Thorne, B., Chee, A., & Lam, W. S. E. (2001). Transnational childhoods: The participation of children in processes of family migration. *Social Problems*, 48(4), 572–591.

Patel, L. (2015). Deservingness: Challenging coloniality in education and migration scholarship. *Association of Mexican American Educators Journal*, 9(3).

Reich, G., & Barth, J. (2012). Immigration restriction in the states: Contesting the boundaries of federalism? *Publius*, 42(3), 422–448.

Rios, V. (2011). *Punished*. NYU Press.

Stephen, L. (2007). *Transborder lives: Indigenous Oaxacans in Mexico, California, and Oregon.* Duke University Press.

Suárez-Orozco, C. (2015). Family separations and reunifications. In C. Suárez-Orozco, M. M. Abo-Zena, & A. K. Marks (Eds.), *Transitions: The development of children of immigrants* (pp. 69–94). New York University Press.

PART II
Issues Impacting Students

4
SHIFTING NATIONAL IDENTITIES AND IMMIGRATION STATUSES

FIGURE 4.1 Sharely and her sister, Nancy, placed their handprints in the cement of the bedroom their father was adding to the new family home (2019).

DOI: 10.4324/9780429340178-6

64 Issues Impacting Students

> When I see [this photo], I feel like I am home. Because it is my home. The handprint has my name and my sister's name. It is mine. My property. No one could take my home away. I would write beneath it: A home of ours. It's like I leave my handprint here in Mexico. It's where I am. The star is because of all the stars in Mexico. You can see the stars here very well because there are not a lot of buildings or light. We have the stars—one point for Mexico.
>
> —*Sharely*

I don't know where I belong. Sometimes I say I'm from Mexico, I have Mexican blood but I have the culture of the US. I feel like a little bit of everything. Sometimes I say neither here nor there.

—*Melchor*

The new mestiza copes by developing a tolerance for contradictions, a tolerance for ambiguity. She learns to be an Indian in a Mexican culture, to be Mexican from an Anglo point of view. She learns to juggle cultures ... Not only does she sustain contradictions, she turns the ambivalence into something else.

—*Anzaldúa, 2012, p. 101*

Transborder students form their identities as they figure out who they are and dream about who they want to become. Their sense of self may differ from the labels that are imposed upon them by external perceptions and by governmental designations as they move across and within borders and countries. Melchor's struggle to self-identity resists an either/or mentality that forces the abandonment of one identity in order to claim another. He sees himself more holistically in some ways, more segmented in others.

Gloria Anzaldúa, a Chicana feminist scholar, reframes borderlands in her seminal book *Borderlands/La Frontera: The New Mestiza*, originally published in 1987. This genre-bending text employs prose and poetry to describe her experiences on the border of Texas and Mexico. She pushed against socially constructed dualities and divisions, demonstrating how they are weaponized against people. Transborder students grapple with the dualities of being Mexican or "American," undocumented or citizens, English or Spanish speakers, Indigenous or mestizo; however, they have lived these realities for most of their lives and therefore have been shaped by them. Anzaldúa sees borders as physical, emotional, cultural and linguistic spaces of tension, growth, and creation, and transborder student identities demonstrate this complexity. National identities are unrooted from geographies of land, but are mapped onto the hearts of those living transborder lives. She affirms that, "Deep in our hearts we believe that being Mexican has nothing to do with which country one lives in. Being Mexican is a state of soul—not one of mind, not one of citizenship" (Anzaldúa, 2012, p. 84).

National citizenship is a formal designation of membership to a country that grants rights and opportunities for those deemed worthy and serves a roadblock for those who are denied and demarcated as "other" (Yuval-Davis, 2007). There are, however, as Anzaldúa explains, varied ways beyond a legal declaration to develop connections to a place. Ong (1996, 1999), for example, conceptualizes cultural citizenship as rooted in an individual's lived experience based on internal factors and feelings of connectivity rather than institutional policies that dictate inclusion or exclusion. This perspective contrasts to the dominant view of citizenship as a political designation based on external factors such as governmental regulations about who "belongs" to a nation via birthright or naturalized citizenship, thereby granting or banning them specific rights and privileges. These binary approaches to citizenship show the disconnect between one's place of birth, where they are deemed citizens, and their place of residence, where they grew up and feel the strongest connection and belonging. As a result, the place transborder students may claim as home may not claim them in return.

The powerful role of a country and its rigid political designations determine belonging via different immigration statuses that are dependent on factors such as birthplace and age. The United States awards citizenship to all those who are born in the country, to those born outside the country to US-citizen parents, and to those who complete the naturalization process as per the 14th Amendment. All US citizens are also designated as US nationals.[1] In contrast, Mexico makes a distinction between nationality and citizenship. Mexico grants citizenship only to individuals aged 18 or older. Article 34 of the Constitución Política de los Estados Unidos Mexicanos notes that citizenship is tied to civic participation, including having the right to vote and being of age to serve in the military. Minors, who make up 40% of Mexico's population, must wait until the age that delineates the start of adulthood to obtain Mexican citizenship (Canché Arteaga, 2012).

In 1998, Mexico began allowing people to apply for doble nacionalidad, which translates literally to double nationality and is widely interpreted in the US to be the same as dual citizenship. However, because Mexican nationals younger than 18 cannot be citizens, the most accurate description of children with such governmental affiliations to both countries would be as US citizens and Mexican nationals. I will use the terms doble nacionalidad and dual citizenship interchangeably because these are the most commonly used labels, but it is important to note that neither is a fully accurate representation of transnational political realities.

While this study emphasizes migration, ethnicity, nationality, and citizenship, other factors certainly influence transborder student identities. These areas can be inclusive of race, gender, class, sexuality, religion, dis/ability, and much more. It is also important to note that geography may intensify or diminish attention to the social and human differences that shape transborder students' self-identities (Compton-Lilly et al., 2017). That said, within the focus of this study will be the aspects of identity that are most closely connected to living a transbordered childhood and adolescence.

Images of Home for Young Transborder Students

FIGURE 4.2 Sharely at her high school in Tlacolula de Matamoros, Oaxaca (2015).

> When I was at school, I would always want to be, trying to fit in. When I was studying in Los Angeles, I didn't feel part of either the state or the people there. It was a different country, a different culture. It was strange for me because I was an immigrant. People would see me and say, "Oh you're Mexican." But here, in this photo, I feel like I am at home. This is my culture, this is me. I'm learning about my culture. I feel like I fit in. Just with the uniform you can tell I'm Mexican. It's me representing my school and my country.
>
> —*Sharely*

Home is a concept with many meanings. There is the fixed notion of home as a stand-alone place of safety (Holloway & Valentine, 2000), something that is often absent in the life of a child on the move. Conversely, viewed through a postcolonial and feminist lens, home is rooted in movement through the connections that are made across different spaces (Gilroy, 1997). In other words, "being grounded is not necessarily about being fixed; being mobile is not necessarily about being detached" (Ahmed et al., 2020, p. 1). This interpretation of "home" is fluid and evolving, a concept that is more aligned with the lives of students living across borders.

Shifting National Identities 67

Describing home can be complex when it spans places and countries. To allow the students a multimodal way to express their views and compare their lives between the US and Mexico, I asked the elementary students to draw pictures to represent their experiences. Per my directions, they divided their pages in two with a US/New York side and Mexico/Oaxaca side. Their pieces are similar in that the sun is present in all the drawings (although not in both places), and they all included themselves and their family members.

FIGURE 4.3 Melany's drawing of Mexico and the US.

Melany drew her life in Mexico with a shining and smiling sun, as well as her home with her mother and father. Nearby she also drew her kindergarten class with a teacher and other students. The scene is very alive. By contrast, the bottom half of the US and specifically New York is sparse; there are no people or sunshine. There is only a multi-story building topped by a flag. When she was asked to describe the US side, she said, "Es que no sé cómo se llama. En la ciudad. Es una bandera de Nueva York" (I don't know what is called. In the city. It's a flag from New York). The Mexico section contains the important people to her. The US section reflects the limited years Melany spent in New York and her accordingly spare memories of living in the country. With little recollections to work with, she recreated what she has seen in movies—the skyscraper and the symbolic flag.

FIGURE 4.4 Axianeydt's drawing comparing life in Mexico and the US.

In Axianeydt's drawing she is outside in both countries. In the US, she is learning to ride a bike with the loving support of her mother; in Mexico, she is riding a horse on her own. Unlike the other students, she included a statement, which translates to: "I want to live with my dad and mom wherever they go, I want the government to help me." Her words show the level of understanding a transborder child of 9 years old has regarding policies that permit or prohibit people to cross national borders. As someone who lives with the consequences of these policies, she also understands that it is the government that creates those policies and has the power to change them. When Axianeydt was asked to explain her drawing, she focused on economic issues rather than the political implications of her quote:

> Es cuando yo recuerdo que mi mamá me enseñó a manejar en Nueva York ... Todo es Nueva York. Porque Nueva York fue mejor que México aquí. Allá hay muchos ponies y acá puro caballo grande. Allá podemos salir a más lugares porque ahí había mucho dinero y como mi papá y mamá trabajaban nos llevaban a los restaurantes y al parque y acá no nos llevan a ningún lugar porque no tiene lana (dinero).
>
> [It's when my mom taught me to ride a bike in New York ... Everything is New York because New York is better than here in Mexico. Over there you see many ponies and here you only see big horses. There, we can go out to more places because there was more money and since my mom and dad worked, they used to take us to restaurants and the park. Here, we can't go anywhere because they don't have any money.]

FIGURE 4.5 Karla's drawing with her father sleeping inside the house in the US/Estabos Unidos (*sic*) and without her father in Oaxaca.

70 Issues Impacting Students

Axianeydt's younger sister, Karla, also divided her drawing with the US on the left and Oaxaca, Mexico, on the right, and put a heart by each location. When she initially showed me her drawing, I noticed her father was missing from the US side, where they were living as a family of five. After I asked her about this, she went back and added her father sleeping inside the house. She said he worked nights so the children would rarely see him during the day because that was when he caught up on his sleep. Their father did not return to Mexico with the children and their mother, so he was not physically present in their lives there, and the sense of separation Karla had felt in the US remained. The reason was different, but the outcome was similar.

Language as Basis for National Identities

When transborder students consider their national identities, it is often language, and specifically the official or dominant de facto language spoken in the country, that connects with their sense of identity. Melany, who was born in New York, was asked if she felt more like a Mexican or a New Yorker. As a 3rd grader she responded, "Los dos, porque a veces un poco en inglés hablo en mi escuela con mis amigos" (Both, because sometimes I speak a little English with my friends at school). Because she lives in Mexico, it can be assumed that she speaks Spanish regularly, so her comment suggests she speaks both languages and thus connects to both countries. However, in the absence of formal English instruction for the remaining years of elementary school, she is likely to speak English less and less over time. As a result, her ties to the US may diminish, if language continues to serve as her primary factor in determining national identity.

Sharely's view of her national identity is also explicitly linked to language:

> I identify myself in the USA like a Mexican-American because I wasn't really into the Spanish culture and because I didn't really speak a lot of Spanish, but I was Mexican too because my parents are Mexican and they speak Spanish so I have that reason to be Mexican. In my school I saw myself more American than Mexican. Now, I consider myself more Mexican because I don't go to school where everything starts with English, everything starts with Spanish so ... I consider myself more Mexican.

Sharely's national identity evolved from a hybrid "Mexican-American" label in the US to solely "Mexican" once she returned to the country where she was born. She connected being Mexican to the Spanish language, which was present in the US through her parents and in Mexico in her schooling. However, as soon as she started school in Mexico—and stayed in Spanish aside from one English class (which was too basic for transborder students with English language practices like Sharely's)—she dropped her American identity.

Sharely and Melany both make a strong connection between national identity and speaking or being around family members who speak the common language of the nation. If this is indeed how transborder students ground their national identities, will they let go of a connection to a country once a language associated with it is no longer a part of their lives? Can they remain connected to the US or Mexico without hearing or speaking English, Spanish or Indigenous languages such as Zapotec? Anzaldúa asserts that "ethnic identity is twin skin to linguistic identity—I am my language. Until I can take pride in my language, I cannot take pride in myself" (2012, p. 81). How language shows up in the life of a transborder student is a window into how they identify themselves.

Additionally, language also partially determines how one is granted or restricted from belonging. Nations reinforce the link between political citizenship and languages, specifically those that hold the highest status or power in their policies. Spanish and English are those languages in Mexico and the US respectively, although neither has granted the languages official status. Both countries also conflate citizenship with proficiency in Spanish or English, disregarding the languages of Indigenous peoples on their land. The US requires anyone seeking naturalized citizenship to take an exam that not only tests their knowledge of US history and government, but also requires them to speak English as well as read and write a few sentences in the language. Mexico's naturalization process, similarly, requires a test of Mexican history and culture as well as evidence of a basic Spanish proficiency. The role of language is not only an external requirement for belonging to a given nation, but an internalized factor transborder students use to gauge their (dis)connection to the US and Mexico.

External Questions and Perceptions

FIGURE 4.6 Karla, left, with her sister, brother, and cousin, riding in their grandfather's truck in Ciénaga de Zimatlán, Oaxaca (2015).

72 Issues Impacting Students

The peers of transborder students often see them as different and ask them to explain themselves. This forces them to describe their national identities and migration histories to classmates, other children in their towns, and even to strangers. Once she and her siblings were in Mexico, Karla said, kids in their class would often inquire about her family's background. "Ellos nos dicen, '¿A donde viviste?' '¿A dónde naciste?'" (They ask us, "Where did you live? Where were you born?"). Given that she, her sister, and her brother had only lived in the US during their early childhood, they don't recall such questions being asked there.

Ricardo experienced these questions in both countries. "First of all," he said, "I would answer officially I am Mexican. Unofficially, I would consider myself to be Latino or Hispanic. [And in the US] I would have said I am Latino." His explanation includes a dichotomy of categories and identities with Mexican as official and Hispanic or Latino as unofficial. Perhaps his "official" designation is tied to political citizenship within a country, which for him is rooted in Mexico. But his "unofficial" designation is connected with being Hispanic or Latino, which is not tied to any specific (national) borders, but is a diaspora that is more closely aligned to his transborder experiences. Interestingly, Ricardo referred to himself as Latino in the US, rather than Mexican, which relates to feeling a connection with people beyond Mexico to those from Latin American who in some ways make up a community in the US. However, it could also be a way to avoid being connected to Mexico, since the country and its citizens are often portrayed and viewed negatively in the US (Shinnar, 2008).

While living in South Carolina, Yauzin felt judged when she said that she was from Mexico; upon her return to the country, she had similar experiences when she spoke about living in the US:

> When I was in the States they would ask me "Where are you from?"… I was embarrassed to say I was Mexican because English people say "Mexican" with a tone that's very aggressive. I said it but I was like, "Oh, God, here it comes." The word for me was very strong.
>
> And when I came here [to Mexico], they would ask me, "Where are you from?" I'd be like, "From Oaxaca." When I lived in Michoacán they'd say, "Really? You're tall and white." I was like, "Really? Am I tall? Am I white?" and they wouldn't believe me. When I came here to Oaxaca, they would ask me … I would say, "I am from la costa." They'd say "You're white and not dark." There is always something about me, my color, my height, or something that doesn't make people happy, I guess.

Although Ricardo didn't elaborate on his aversion to saying he was Mexican in the US, Yauzin braced herself for the reactions she received when she revealed she was from Mexico. Nonetheless, despite her anticipation of negative responses, she continued to state she was Mexican. Once she returned to the country, she became the target of another form of judgment, one based on her place of birth and her appearance, as she is taller and lighter-skinned than what some Oaxacans associate with people who are from the coastal town where she was born. Being questioned about her background across nations led to uncomfortable, difficult, and unavoidable conversations. From a lens of borderlands theory, this highlights how "oppressions are not ranked nor are they conceptualized as static; rather they are recognized as fluid systems that take on different forms and nuances depending on the context" (Cantú & Hurtado, 2012, p. 7). The transborder students in this study were constantly in a position of navigating their changing contexts and responding to the external perceptions and questions imposed upon them.

Internalizing an Undocumented Immigrant Identity in the US

> Pues yo tengo una opinión de que todos en la vida queremos ser felices pero a veces no se da esa oportunidad. Así que yo tengo ese sueño, that dream, de poder regresar a donde yo vivía en Los Angeles o en cualquier parte para poder por lo menos visitar, para recordar mi vida de pequeña.
>
> [Well, I have an opinion that everyone in life wants to be happy, but sometimes that opportunity is not given. So I have this dream, to be able to go back to where I used to live in Los Angeles or anywhere to at least visit, to remember my life as a child.]
>
> —*Sharely*

Crossing international borders to live in a new country is a life-changing event that is woven into one's identity. But how one views being an immigrant is often different from how they are perceived, first as newcomers and eventually as long-term members of a nation. For minors, being an immigrant in the US—especially an undocumented immigrant—is something they come to understand over time through discussions, observations, and experiences. And the freedom to travel was one aspect of her limiting immigration status that Sharely strived for but also realized may not be easily attained. But these impositions may also lead to "transing symbolic, ideological, and physical spaces" (Galván, 2011, p. 552). Anzaldúa explains, "if going home is denied to me I will have to stand and claim my own space, making a new culture—*una cultura mestiza*—with my own lumber, my own bricks, and mortar and my own feminist architecture" (2012, p 44).

Melchor and the other secondary transborder students were all brought to the US in the first years of their lives. Their time in Mexico was not a part of their memories; the US was all they knew. However, their status as undocumented left their futures in the country uncertain. Melchor explained, "My parents told me I didn't have papers, which means I didn't have rights too. They told me to enjoy life here while we have it because we never know when we can go to Mexico and you can miss all this." This reality, which some parents and families choose to be very open about and others shield from children, led Melchor to realize that being an immigrant without papers meant he must be prepared for a life in either country. And his place of residence would not necessarily be a choice that he or his family would make.

FIGURE 4.7 Sharely, center, with her sister, Nancy, and her father, Alberto, during the construction of their home in San Juan, Guelavía, Oaxaca, Mexico (2017).

Research has shown that "the effects of unauthorized status on development across the lifespan are uniformly negative, with millions of US children and youth at risk of lower educational performance, economic stagnation, blocked mobility, and ambiguous belonging. In all, the data suggest an alarming psychosocial formation" (Suárez-Orozco et al., 2011, p. 461). Sharely felt a big difference between being an undocumented immigrant in the US and being a retornada from the US in Mexico:

> I could've been happy being in Los Angeles, if there was no pressure like that. And I am happy here [in Oaxaca] because I don't have to go out and be worried with the police. I want to stay here in Mexico because this is where I belong and I feel this is where I'm supposed to be.

Being an undocumented immigrant is akin to feeling like you have done something wrong, says Sharely, when in fact surviving and thriving are the reasons for your family's journey. Even as a child Sharely was always hyper-aware of her actions because her family lived under continual fear of authorities such as the police and ICE. This reality and burden did not align with Sharely's perception of what it meant to be an immigrant. Happiness and freedom were critical to her expectations for living a dignified life, but became the antithesis of her experiences. This ultimately pushed her to forgo this part of her identity and live in a way that allowed her to remove the veil of fear that was imposed upon her. She recovered her sense of freedom when she returned to Mexico, where she could live more fully and freely.

The freedoms of immigrants were further limited after the events of September 11, 2001. This day has played a central role in the recent history of the US in further framing immigrants of color as criminals. Antonio, Yauzin's father, was living in the US at the time of the attacks. He recalls that prior to 9/11 "todo indocumentado estaba trabajando bien, no había ningún problema. Ese día cambió todo y más para los indocumentados, fue lo más drástico que hubo" (Every undocumented person was working well, there were no problems. That day, everything changed, especially for us. It was the most drastic thing of all). Yauzin notes the irony of the impact on undocumented immigrants, who played no role in the attacks:

> ¿Los terroristas que cometieron el acto en el 9/11 entraron por avión entonces quiere decir que tenían visa, no? ¿Ellos los dejaron entrar, no? Y nosotros, que no nos dieron visa, pasamos ilegalmente no somos terroristas, fíjate a quién le das visa y a quién no.
>
> [The terrorists from the 9/11 tragedy entered by airplane. That meant they had visas, right? They were let in, right? And we didn't get any visas, we crossed illegally, we are not the terrorists. Pay attention to who you give visas to.]

This moment intensified what is referred to as *crimmigration*, the meshing of immigration and criminal law.

> Both criminal and immigration law are, at their core, systems of inclusion and exclusion. They are similarly designed to determine whether and how to include individuals as members of society or exclude them from it. Both create insiders and outsiders. Both are designed to create distinct categories of people—innocent versus guilty, admitted versus excluded or, as some say, "legal" versus "illegal." Viewed in that light, perhaps it is not surprising that these two areas of law have become entwined.
>
> *—Stumpf, 2006, p. 380*

Crimmigration after 9/11 was heightened by the 2003 formation of the US Immigration and Customs Enforcement (ICE) as an arm of the Division of Homeland Security receiving one-fifth of its budget (Henderson, 2011). Since then, ICE has been responsible for terrorizing, detaining, and deporting hundreds of thousands of people yearly. The organization has a central role in pushing the immigrant-as-criminal narrative. Some immigrants internalize this identity. Others enact their "complex personhood" (Gordon, 2008), which for undocumented youth "includes excitement, revulsion, resentment, and relief at being marginally seen by the state, is itself an act of resistance worth noting…in a

76 Issues Impacting Students

common struggle for control over varied forms of capital and self-definition" (Patel & Sánchez Ares, 2014, p. 149). Or, as in the case of Yauzin—who returned to Mexico immediately after completing high school—some evade this identity entirely by leaving the country as an act of resistance coupled with refusal.

Mixed-status Families

> I am Mexican, I was born in Oaxaca, but I love speaking English and I feel more American than Mexican.
>
> —*Brayan*

> I am from the USA, but I love speaking Spanish. I love both languages, but I love Spanish because I speak more Spanish.
>
> —*Cristopher, Brayan's US-born brother*

All of the secondary transborder students had younger US-born siblings. This made them mixed-status families in both countries. In the US, the parents and older siblings were undocumented Mexican nationals; the younger siblings were US citizens and who could become dual citizens of both countries, while the rest of the family only had Mexican nationality and/or citizenship. Upon returning to Mexico, those born there were no longer undocumented as they had been in the US, and the US-born children retained citizenship privileges across the US and Mexico. Brayan clearly saw this difference between himself and his younger brother. "He can go back as fast as he can," Brayan said. "He has more opportunities just being American citizen. But it doesn't bother me because he's my brother."

The irony of these political citizenship designations given by countries is that they do not match the lived realities of the transborder children. As Brayan explains in the opening quote of this section, he "feel[s] more American than Mexican." Compared to his brother, Cristopher, he spent more time living and going to school in the US and is more comfortable speaking English. On the other hand, Cristopher spent less time in the US, had less time in US schools and struggles to speak English in comparison to his older brother. He also feels less American even though he is a US citizen, highlighting the disconnect of his political and cultural citizenship (Ong, 1996, 1999). However, these lived experiences are not factored into determining who is granted US citizenship, thereby denying Brayan the opportunity to align his cultural citizenship with his political citizenship.

Although Brayan doesn't resent the different opportunities his US-citizen brother has in regard to traveling or living in the US, he does take issue with the difference between the way the US and Mexican governments manage access to both countries: "In my opinion, it's not fair that only US citizens are allowed to go back to the US … For example, Mexico allows American people to come to Mexico, I don't understand why we can't cross over." Brayan and the family of

Alberta saw this firsthand in my interactions with them. While I was living in Mexico for six months, I traveled back to the US twice for meetings and conferences. The trips involved nothing more than purchasing flights and having my US passport in hand. I did not have to pay an application fee for a tourist visa and await an answer that may likely be negative to return to Mexico. This difference was not lost on Brayan, as his comments reveal. It was also pointed out at a gathering at Alberta's house; a family friend, learning that I had been to the US and back since the last time she saw me, said, "Oh, I forgot, it's so easy for you." Cristopher, Brayan's brother, has the same privilege I have, provided that he or his family have the finances to purchase a flight. If Alberta's friend had been from a higher socio-economic status, she may have been able to receive a tourist visa to travel freely between the US and Mexico, but even then, the application process and cost still differs from the experience as a US citizen. This highlights the differences in rights between US and Mexican citizens in general, as well as between Mexicans who live in poverty and even the middle class, compared to those with greater means.

In spite of being aware of the inequitable systems, Brayan still held out hope that he would be able to return to the US without citizenship. His plan was as follows: "When he [Cristopher] turns 18 and I turn 21, both of us will return … He can get me and my mom papers so that we can also go to the United States and visit. One day we'll return." Brayan's plan is for Cristopher to use his US citizenship to return to the US and then petition for him and his mother to be granted permission to live in the US. While this is a viable approach for an adult US citizen to bring their family over, there are a few obstacles. First, a US citizen cannot petition for a family member until they are 21 years of age. Also, the timeframe for getting a case processed by US Citizenship and Immigration Services (USCIS) can take years. The average wait time to receive an answer to sponsor a parent is 1–2 years while it increased to 10–12 years for a sibling (USCIS, n.d.).

Similar to Brayan, Sharely's US-citizen sibling, Nancy, has different opportunities due to her place of birth. Their mother, Tere, took note of what having mixed-status children meant in Mexico and the US. She reflected on the support she was given by the federal government in the US for Nancy as she was denied those very same supports for Sharely: "Con Nancy me daban más ayuda, por ejemplo la guardería, el food stamp, algo que se le hizo muy difícil de entender a Sharely" (With Nancy they gave me more help. For example, daycare, food stamps. That was hard for Sharely to understand). The differences did not go away when they returned to Mexico, but continued to stand out between Sharely and Nancy:

Con Sharely me gustaría regresar para allá porque sé que ella quiere estudiar y allá puede. Pero ahorita está muy difícil la frontera y ya no quiero arriesgarme, aunque el corazón quiere ya no se puede.

78 Issues Impacting Students

> [I would love to go back over there with Sharely because I know she would love to go to school there. The problem is that the crossing is very dangerous now and I do not want to put our lives at risk. Even if the heart wants it, it's impossible.]
>
> —*Tere, Sharely's mother*

Tere gets to the root of the issue when it comes to belonging and rights in her statement about what that heart wants. While political citizenship only takes into account factors of time and place of birth, cultural citizenship is rooted in the heart and soul, and starts with an individual's sense of self and belonging. Still, without a match in political citizenship, the individual is denied the chance to live an integrated life, one in which their sense of self aligns with the policies and regulations of the country or countries in which they reside.

DACA and Mixed-status Families

Yauzin's family became mixed-status after President Obama announced the Deferred Action for Childhood Arrivals (DACA) program in 2012. Yauzin would have qualified for this program had she stayed in the US, but because she returned to Mexico in 2009, she was ineligible. However, her younger brother Tony remained in the US and became a DACA recipient. He received a Social Security number for working purposes and a stay from deportation, which had to be renewed every two years. Tony made the decision to stay in the US after everyone in his immediate family returned either due to refusal for Yauzin, deportation for their father and coercion for their mother. Given that Tony arrived in the US at the age of six, which was three years younger than Yauzin, his connection to Mexico was more fleeting. Yauzin expressed some discomfort in her brother's decision:

> I didn't want to go back [to the US] for fun, I wanted to go back to see my little brother because he didn't want to come back, he says that he feels American. He feels that Mexico is not his country anymore because he doesn't remember it ... I was going [back to Mexico] ... to set an example for him because at first I really wanted him to come back to Mexico to study here, but now I understand his position and I respect it.

Yauzin eventually came to understand her brother's choice to stay in the US under the temporary protections of DACA. But being part of a mixed-status family that lived in two countries led her to feel she needed to justify her decision to return to her brother and others who viewed being back in Mexico as a sign of failure. She set out to prove just the opposite:

> I just want to keep proving to myself that I can do anything I want and also be an example for my brother ... I see that he has DACA approved, but

because of the money he's not able to go to college yet. And I want to tell him that if one day he decides to come back to Mexico it's OK ... I just want to prove to him that not all Mexicans are a failure just because they decide to come back to their country, [it doesn't] mean they are going to get stuck there. I keep traveling and keep studying and prove that I can do many, many things.

Living as a mixed-status family in one country is complex, but it is even more so when family members, and especially siblings, live between nations. The ability to travel internationally and attend higher education are just two areas that can set siblings apart. Additionally, there are varied views about decisions that are made to either stay in a country where one's rights are limited due to immigration status or return to their place of birth. With the latter option, the perception may be that one will have more rights but fewer opportunities. However, the case of Yauzin—who earned a bachelor's degree in Mexico and became a teacher—shows that is not always the case.

The Price of US Citizenship Rights

FIGURE 4.8 Karla, center, with her mother, Alberta, and her brother, Zayd, in Ciénaga de Zimatlán, Oaxaca, after riding home from school (2018).

> Every time we left the house it was like a fun adventure, with my brother and I together, competing (on our bikes) with my mom. It was so much fun.
> —*Karla*

No pueden regresar si no hay pasaporte.
[They can't go back without a passport.]

—*Alberta*

All US citizens are provided social security cards at no cost, while only 42% of US citizens are passport holders (Henderson, 2019). Passports, which are needed for travel outside the country, are not given automatically and require additional steps and costs. Some families are unable to obtain a passport for their US-born children prior to leaving for Mexico, especially if their departure is unplanned (i.e., by deportation), even though their children will need a valid passport to return to the US. The cost of the process (at least $80 USD per child) can be an obstacle, as can the fear of engaging with the application process that appears intrusive and overwhelming, especially for undocumented people.

Alberta obtained passports for her three US-born children prior to leaving the US. However, if children are under 16—as hers were—a passport is only valid for five years, as opposed to ten years for everyone else. Once her children were in Mexico they had a shorter window of opportunity to use their US passport to return to the US or travel elsewhere. Because Alberta lives in a community with a large migrant population, the town's president hired someone to help families with US-born children obtain or renew US passports:

> Elizabeth te ayuda en buena parte en el papeleo porque si yo voy directamente al consulado americano me pide muchas cosas y ahorita con esta ayuda que nos llegó aquí con Elizabeth es menos, nada más que como no están nuestros esposos nos cuesta más trabajo porque nos piden una carta de él donde nos tiene que dar permiso porque él es el papá y notariada y tiene que ser firmada de allá de Estados Unidos.
>
> [Elizabeth helps us with the passport process. It is much easier with her because if I were to do it on my own, the American Consulate would ask me for so many things. However, the process for me is a little difficult because my husband is in the US and he has to send me a notarized letter of consent.]
>
> —*Alberta*

This support helped Alberta save the time and the expense of traveling to the closest US Consulate, which was in Mexico City, a six-hour bus ride from Oaxaca. Still, she had to pay to renew her children's passports, which came to $1,400 Mexican pesos per passport. For some US citizens living in Mexico, the fee may be prohibitive. For people like Alberta, who are unemployed, the cost—multiplied by three for each of her children—is a barrier to their rights as US citizens to live in the US.

Proof of citizenship is not sufficient to allow US citizens to (re)enter the country. The rights of US-born citizens living in other countries are only granted at a financial cost that may be out of reach for low-income families. In effect, the

US government only allows transborder US-born children to return and live in their birthplace at a price.

Doble Nacionalidad/Dual Citizenship

The ability for individuals to obtain citizenship in more than one country has been a growing global trend over the last three decades. Harpaz and Mateos define this phenomenon as strategic citizenship:

> a new field that examines these changes in three domains: (a) acquisition strategies (for example, citizenship reacquisition on the basis of ancestry or ethnicity); (b) instrumental uses (for example, citizenship as insurance policy or as a premium passport) and (c) perceptions (for example, citizenship as a commodity, status symbol or an ethnic marker).
>
> —*Harpaz & Mateos, 2019, p. 844*

Since 1998 anyone born in the US to a parent with Mexican citizenship can also receive Mexican nationality. It is not automatically granted, however. An application, which includes the child's and parent(s) birth certificate, is required, in addition to a fee of about $300 Mexican pesos or $15 US dollars. This form of governmental citizenship allows people to more easily live, study, work, and own property in both nations, but it also comes at a price.

In this study only the elementary transborder students and the younger siblings of the secondary students were able to receive doble nacionalidad, a concept they would understand more thoroughly as they got older. Axianeydt said that for her doble nacionalidad meant "poder hablar en inglés y español" (being able to speak both Spanish and English). This language-nation connection is a framework that other transborder students used to dis/connect themselves from one nationality or the other.

For the parents, doble nacionalidad took on a very different meaning, one connected with their children's present and future. Emanuel, the father of Melany, sees it as a safety net "to make their life easier someday. We don't know if we have a little problem [in Mexico] the economy is not well for us, they got another option." Alberta elaborated on the greater choices and opportunities this status could offer her children as they get older:

> Para mi significa mucho que mis hijos tengan doble nacionalidad porque ellos pueden entrar y salir cuando ellos quieran y tienen la oportunidad de estudiar en otro país. Ahorita ellos opinan que quieren estar en México porque están chiquitos y se sienten libres, pero ya cuando estén más grandes van a pensar diferente y me van a decir que se van y no hay riesgo de que va a pasar algo. Como nosotros que nos arriesgamos y ellos desde que suben en el avión llegan a su país como si nada y con la ganancia de que a uno de inmigrante te discriminan y ellos tienen un papel que diga "yo nací aquí."

[It means a lot to me that my children have dual nationality. Because they are able to enter and leave Mexico or the US whenever they want to and they also have the opportunity to study anywhere they want. Right now they want to live here in Mexico because they are young and have a better sense of freedom here. But when they are older they might change their mind and say mom, we are leaving. At that point there's less chances of something happening to them, for example like us, we risked everything and they will not have to go through that because they can just get on a plane and be in their country of origin, as if they would have never left. They also have the benefit of a paper that proves that they were born there because sometimes as an immigrant you are discriminated against.]

FIGURE 4.9 Alberta doing Karla's hair the day of her 6th grade graduation (2018).

Both families see doble nacionalidad/dual citizenship as a way to ensure a life for their children with more opportunities and fewer risks. Alberta and Emanuel believe their children's status affects the areas of education, economics, and migration. Given that economic opportunities in Mexico are limited, the option of their children having more choices in the US comforts them. Economic factors also impact education. High school, for example, is free in the US, but comes at a cost in Mexico. And while there are scholarships for higher education in both countries, financial aid is available for US college students who are citizens. Dual nationality ultimately allows citizens to more freely live, study, work and travel between the two, therefore avoiding making a choice between one country or another. Alberta points out her children can do this without the risks that so many migrants face in their journey to the US, from riding atop a freight train where they may lose their life, to drowning in a river, to being robbed or sexually assaulted to battling harsh desert conditions. Being able to purchase a plane ticket and safely travel between countries, to be with family on both sides of the border, evades these very real risks and diminishes the competing dualities of a transborder life. The children can enjoy one life that transcends the border instead of enduring what feels like two distinct lives separated by one border.

Identity Anchors Beyond Nationality

While place of birth or place of residency can be a central factor of identity, there are many more aspects of one's background and experiences that affect how transborder students identify at their core. Writing about religion as a stabilizing force for displaced youth in their identity formation, Zine (2001) theorizes anchors as "a means to mediate the dissonance and challenge of living in environments that were laced with conflicting cultural values and practice" (p. 402). For Erik, who spent most of his childhood in the US and returned to Mexico as an adolescent, that anchor was soccer. It consistently grounded him in both countries and allowed him to be his full self.

I asked Erik to create an artifact that symbolized his life across the two countries that had been his home at different points of his life. While the elementary transborder students drew pictures of their binational experiences, he did not feel comfortable drawing. Instead he created a model of a soccer field that was divided by a line with the US and Mexican flags planted on each side. In between were two players, apparently on opposing teams, positioned on the halfway line—a line whose placement suggests a parallel to the Mexican-US border.

FIGURE 4.10 Erik's representation of living between the US and Mexico.

84 Issues Impacting Students

Erik's life between both countries has also been full of struggles, but it was soccer that allowed him to overcome some of those obstacles and to be himself, as he was more easily able to fit in and make friends in both contexts.

Erik explained the moment after being back in Mexico that finally gave him a sense of groundedness and belonging:

> In the towns, when you go to the US and you come back, all eyes are on you. I felt weird. At first, I didn't get out of my house a lot, I stayed like that for like three months. I remember telling my mom that I wanted to come back to the US [because] I didn't feel comfortable, I didn't have any friends here. She was like, "you'll start going out." I have a friend that started taking me out of my house and then there was like a soccer tournament my uncle invited me to and we started talking and hanging out and that's when I started feeling more comfortable.

While soccer has been an anchor for Erik across countries, there are many other possible anchors that are related to sports and other activities that may be central in the lives of transborder students. For instance, Axianeydt made art, and specifically drawings of animals and then anime characters—a type of Japanese animation—as a stabilizing force across contexts. These anchors allow transborder students to keep a part of themselves consistent and thriving regardless of where they may find themselves in the world.

FIGURE 4.11 Axianeydt with her anime drawings in her bedroom in Ciénaga de Zimatlán, Oaxaca (2017).

Comparison Across Levels

Transborder students vary significantly in their identities related to the countries they have called home at various points in their lives as they negotiate internal dis/connections, external perceptions and treatment, and governmental designations. The elementary students in this study are all US citizens by birth and received doble nacionalidad by way of their parents' place of birth. Their political citizenship provides them with rights within and between both countries. Yet their limited time in the US and discomfort with English limits their emotional connection to the country. It is an aspect of their lives they do not openly share with their peers. And due to the undocumented status of their parents in the US, they still live with the inequities of political factors as they deal with family separations.

The Mexican-born secondary students in this study have a conflicting sense of identity when it comes to political and cultural citizenship, especially when compared to their US-born younger siblings, whose experiences are more aligned to those of the elementary students. The secondary students are Mexican nationals, but they spent their formative childhood years in the US, where they were immersed in the culture and English language in schools. However, they were never able to fully belong due to their undocumented status. This was somewhat evident as they were growing up in the US, but became even clearer when their mixed-status families returned to Mexico. There, they learned that while their younger siblings could live in either or in both countries, they faced many obstacles in order to visit or return to the US, in spite of feeling more connected to the country. These experiences have allowed them to understand the nuances of immigration law, which they navigate with great skill as young people in mixed-status families.

The transborder students at the tertiary level in the study saw themselves as identifying in ways that vacillate between Mexican, American, Latinx, and Hispanic, or a combination of these national, ethnic and pan-ethnic labels. Their connection to one or more identities often depended on whom they were speaking to and where they were located, nationally and locally. Regardless of how they identified internally, they could see how immigration status, coupled with their racial background and Mexican heritage, positioned them as inferior in the US. But they worked to disprove those harmful and violent perceptions, just as they looked for belonging and connection in ways that went beyond immigration and nationality.

All three groups of transborder students are at different stages of becoming, partly as children and youth, but also as they make sense of their lives across borders. Anzaldúa captures their state in what she terms Nepantla:

> [Nepantla] is a Nahuatl word for the space between two bodies of water, the space between two worlds. It is a limited space, a space where you are not this or that but where you are changing. You haven't gotten into the new

identity yet and haven't left the old identity behind either—you are in a kind of transition ... It is very awkward, uncomfortable and frustrating to be in that Nepantla because you are in the midst of transformation.

—Anzaldúa, 2012, p. 276

Note

1 The only group of people who are US nationals without US citizenship are those born in US territories such as American Samoa and Swains Island.

References

Ahmed, S., Castada, C., Fortier, A. M., & Sheller, M. (Eds.). (2020). *Uprootings/regroundings: Questions of home and migration*. Routledge.

Anzaldúa, G. (2012). *Borderlands/la frontera: The new mestiza* (4th ed.). aunt lute.

Canché Arteaga, L. E. (2012). El niño y adolescente como ciudadano mexicano. *Boletín Mexicano de Derecho Comparado*, 45(135), 1023–1061. www.scielo.org.mx/scielo.php?script=sci_arttext&pid=S0041-86332012000300004&lng=es&tlng=es.

Cantú, N. E. & Hurtado, A. (2012). Introduction. In G. Anzaldúa, *Borderlands/La frontera: The new mestiza* (4th ed.) (pp. 3–13). aunt lute.

Compton-Lilly, C., Papoi, K., Venegas, P., Hamman, L., & Schwabenbauer, B. (2017). Intersectional identity negotiation: The case of young immigrant children. *Journal of Literacy Research*, 49(1), 115–140.

Galván, R.T. (2011). Chicana transborder vivencias and autoherteorías: Reflections from the field. *Qualitative Inquiry*, 17(6), 552–557.

Gilroy, P. (1997). *Diaspora and the detours of identity*. In K. Woodward (Ed.), *Identity and Difference*. Sage/Open University Press.

Gordon, A. F. (2008). *Ghostly matters: Haunting and the sociological imagination*. University of Minnesota Press.

Harpaz, Y., & Mateos, P. (2019). Strategic citizenship: negotiating membership in the age of dual nationality. *Journal of Ethnic and Migration Studies*, 45 (6), 843–857. doi:10.1080/1369183X.2018.1440482.

Henderson, T. J. (2011). *Beyond borders: A history of Mexican migration to the United States* (Vol. 13). John Wiley & Sons.

Henderson, P. (2019, January 6). More than 42 percent of U.S. citizens have passports. *Courier*. https://www.ntacourier.com/index.php/node/541.

Holloway, S. L., & Valentine, G. (2000). Spatiality and the new social studies of childhood. *Sociology*, 34(4), 763–783.

Ong, A. (1996). Cultural citizenship as subject-making: Immigrants negotiate racial and cultural boundaries in the United States. *Current Anthropology*, 37 (5), 737–762.

Ong, A. (1999). *Flexible citizenship: The cultural logics of transnationality*. Duke University Press.

Patel, L., & Sánchez Ares, R. (2014). The politics of coming out undocumented. In E. Tuck & K. W. Yang (Eds.), *Youth resistance research and theories of change* (pp. 139–152). Routledge.

Shinnar, R. S. (2008). Coping with negative social identity: The case of Mexican immigrants. *The Journal of Social Psychology*, 148(5), 553–576.

Stumpf, J. (2006). The crimmigration crisis: Immigrants, crime, and sovereign power. *American University Law Review*, 56 (2) 367–419.

Suárez-Orozco, C., Yoshikawa, H., Teranishi, R., & Suárez-Orozco, M. (2011). Growing up in the shadows: The developmental implications of unauthorized status. *Harvard Educational Review*, 81 (3), 438–473.

USCIS (n.d.). Check case processing times. https://egov.uscis.gov/processing-times/.

Yuval-Davis, N. (2007). Intersectionality, citizenship and contemporary politics of belonging. *Critical Review of International Social and Political Philosophy*, 10(4), 561–574.

Zine, J. (2001). Muslim youth in Canadian schools: Education and the politics of religious identity. *Anthropology & Education Quarterly*, 32(4), 399–423.

5
LANGUAGE LEARNING, UNLEARNING, AND RELEARNING

FIGURE 5.1 Sharely, preparing to speak in Tlacolula de Matamoros, Oaxaca, during a discussion about families who have returned to Oaxaca from the United States (2015).

My first language is English and then Spanish and I understand Zapotec.
—*Sharely*

DOI: 10.4324/9780429340178-7

Students who live and learn between the US and Mexico develop rich and varied language practices as they navigate complex linguistic landscapes shaped by family, communities, schooling, economies, and power. The linguistic repertoires of the students in this study include features of Spanish, English, and—because they have families rooted in Oaxaca, Mexico—Zapotec, the predominant Indigenous language of that state. Their language practices are closely connected to their cultures, which can be mapped onto the places with which they come into contact. These students' transborder realities differ from those of multilinguals who either reside in one primary location or experience migration as a linear, one-way trajectory. Policies, power, and people also mitigate the language practices of transborder students, who are in a perpetual state of language learning and language loss throughout their migrations.

Communication takes place through languaging, a verb used to denote what one does rather than what they possess (García, 2009). Specifically, it's "a process of making meaning and shaping knowledge and experience through language" by accessing one's complete internal language system or idiolect (Swain, 2006, p. 98). Feliciano, Melchor's father, explains his practices with a focus on how each language connects to a part of his identity and his lived experiences across borders. It is the totality of how he languages that makes him whole and proud:

> Hopefully people don't lose their roots, their culture, or their native tongue. It's very important to be able to speak three languages, it's something to be proud of. English is a language used worldwide … [it] can help you find a job anywhere you go … the second one for me would be Spanish, here in Mexico. I feel very proud to speak Spanish just as much as speaking Zapotec … the language that our people, our ancestors spoke … No one speaks Zapotec but us. We can technically say that we are trilingual because I understand some English, Spanish, and I am fluent in Zapotec.
>
> —*Feliciano*

Melchor's family speaks three languages under one roof, depending on the people involved and the purpose of the conversation. Some examples of interactions across languages might include the following:

- parents speak Zapotec to each other;
- parents speak Spanish to children;
- US-raised children speak English to each other; and
- US-raised children speak Spanish to Mexican-born sibling.

This is, of course, a rather simplified breakdown of one family's language practices. It does not show how translanguaging, the dynamic and flexible use of languages, happens within conversations. For example, when speaking in Zapotec to one another, the parents may select features of English for topics related to the US, and in

Spanish for concepts or terms for which Zapotec may not have a word. Also, while the parents do not speak to the children in Zapotec, their conversations are opportunities for the children to hear the language and build their receptive abilities. The US-raised children feel more comfortable speaking English together because that is what they did in the US, but as their Spanish experience grows in Mexico, the language becomes a more prominent part of their repertoire and a more common aspect of their communicative practice, even with each other.

The next section examines how each language plays a role in the home, community, and school experiences of transborder students and families. It also explores how students value the various features of their linguistic repertoires, values that differ depending on geography (both across and within countries) and external hierarchies of power that are attached to languages and their speakers that may become internalized or instigate a sense of resistance.

Diidx Zah (Zapotec)[1]

Zapotec is a group of languages from the Oto-Manguean language family, although colloquially it is often used to describe any one of the languages in the family. Zapotec is one of Oaxaca's 16 official languages, although with more than 50 varieties, not all speakers of Zapotec can understand one another. A logo-syllabic writing system was used by the Zapotec people as early as 600 BCE. During the Spanish colonial period that began in 1521 and lasted for about 300 years, there was a shift to an alphabetic writing system that led to key documents being translated, as multimodal texts that used the logo-syllabic system were destroyed.

Two of the three families in this study who live in or near Tlacolula include Zapotec as part of their linguistic repertoires. Melchor's and Sharely's grandparents speak the language almost exclusively. Their parents are fluent in Zapotec, but are also comfortable in Spanish. Melchor and Sharely are able to understand a little Zapotec and are open to continuing to learn it. For them, cyclical migration served as a barrier and opportunity to develop Zapotec. When they were in the US they encountered very few speakers of the language. However, once they returned to their villages in Oaxaca and reunited with their grandparents, opportunities to learn Zapotec increased.

Intra- and international migration have both affected how Zapotec has evolved. The oppression of Indigenous peoples has caused economic struggles that have pushed them out of their villages and into cities in Mexico and the US in search of work (Cruz-Manjarrez, 2013). As a result, Indigenous peoples have had to learn Spanish and/or English, sometimes at the cost of their home languages. Meanwhile, there is widespread discrimination against people who are viewed as or identify with Indigenous peoples and languages (Heidbrink, 2020; Perez et al., 2016). In spite of the desire to pass on their linguistic roots, some families may discourage or limit opportunities for their children to speak Zapotec or other Indigenous languages as a way to protect them from discrimination among peers

FIGURE 5.2 Sharely, left, with her grandmother, Margarita, and her sister, Nancy, near their home in San Juan Guelavía, Oaxaca (2017).

in school or in the workforce as adults (López-Gopar, 2016). Yet Zapotec speakers have persisted in their language use and resistance against these detrimental ideologies. Therefore, Zapotec speakers experience complex and contradictory feelings, including pride in their Indigenous heritage and language, as well as shame associated with that aspect of their identity.

Views of Zapotec Across and Within Borders

People in the US generally assume that anyone from Mexico speaks Spanish and only Spanish. Anyone who has spent their life in the US or only visited the tourist resorts of Mexico generally knows little about the Indigenous languages that still thrive in Mexico, especially in states such as Oaxaca and Chiapas, where native communities continue to speak languages such as Zapotec, Mixtec, and Tzotzil. While there is literature about Mexican-origin Indigenous students in US schools (Mesinas & Perez, 2016; Valdiviezo et al., 2014; Vásquez, 2019; Velasco, 2014), indigeneity is still off the radar for many who identify Mexico with the one-nation, one-language ideology.

In Mexico, however, and especially in Oaxaca, there is an awareness of Indigenous languages, but Indigenous speakers are seen as intellectually and culturally inferior (Sánchez, 2018). These views may not be stated explicitly, but are relayed implicitly through media, school curricula, and the absence of Indigenous languages and their speakers in positions of power in broader Mexican society.

92 Issues Impacting Students

Indigenous peoples may hide their language, culture, and ethnicity as a way to protect against deficit-oriented ideologies (López Hernández, 2002). Even though Zapotec is widely used in Tlacolula, students do not always admit to speaking the language. Rafael Vásquez (2015) found that many students in Tlacolula did not initially identify as Zapotec speakers, even though the language was part of their home and community life. Melchor, for example, did not readily talk about the role of Zapotec in his family. Only after multiple conversations did he acknowledge that he has a basic understanding of the language: "I understand some of the words, but I can't speak it." When asked if he'd be interested in learning Zapotec, he responded, "Well, not really, because I don't see it like a benefit. The languages I really want to learn [are] French and Portuguese. I want to be more than trilingual." While Melchor didn't value Zapotec (the primary language of his grandparents), he thought a language like French or Portuguese would be more useful given they are spoken more widely. However, after multiple conversations about the value of Zapotec, Melchor eventually developed an interest in learning more:

> A veces sí quiero hablar más en zapoteco pero a veces digo que no, ¿para qué me sirve? Pero luego digo que sí para comunicarme con mis abuelos que su lengua natal es el zapoteco.
>
> [Sometimes I do wish I spoke more Zapotec, but sometimes not really because I don't see the point but sometimes I think I could use it to speak to my grandparents, whose native language is Zapotec.]

Brayan's family did not speak Zapotec, and similar to Melchor's initial reaction, he saw no reason to learn it in spite of being surrounded by speakers of the language in his community and school. Brayan's views align with dominant societal messages. In Mexico and other Latin American nations, the prevailing model of intercultural bilingual education or educación bilingüe intercultural features the acquisition of Spanish alongside the Indigenous language and culture, but only for Indigenous students. These programs that were initially one-way had the potential to reinforce that Indigenous communities need to learn Spanish, but Indigenous languages have little value to those Spanish monolinguals as they did not receive this model of education (López, 2006).

Sharely, on the other hand, always held a positive connection to Diidx zah (a variety of Zapotec). The language is commonly spoken in her town, a rural community of 3,000 people about 20 minutes by car from her school in Tlacolula:

> El zapoteco en mi pueblo es el lenguaje primero, ese lenguaje es el que hablaron primero nuestros ancestros. Así que es un lenguaje muy bonito y que no se debe perder ya que es un lenguaje que no muchos lo tiene, así que en mi pueblo, lo que hace es tratar de conservar ese lenguaje. En mi familia lo hablamos, bueno mis papás lo hablan, ellos hablan en zapoteco y les

entiendo porque ya con el tiempo el zapoteco ya se va formulando en tu cabeza y lo vas aprendiendo más.

[Zapotec is the first language in my hometown; the language our ancestors spoke first. It is a beautiful language that should not go extinct. In my hometown, what we do is preserve the language. My family speaks Zapotec; when my parents speak it, I understand what they are saying. With time Zapotec sticks to your head and you can learn it more.]

FIGURE 5.3 The wedding of Sharely's aunt, Elena, in San Juan Guelavía, Oaxaca, where Zapotec culture and ceremonies remain strong (2015).

Sharely's positive view of Zapotec, which contradicts the anti-Indigenous views that are prevalent on a macro-level, makes her an outlier. It could be that Indigenous communities serve as a buffer against outside perceptions, and that Zapotec is a form of resistance against these linguistically oppressive forces.

Zapotec in Schools

In the US "Indigenous children have been ignored, silenced and assimilated under the 'Mexican' umbrella and on the hidden side of modernity, and colonial" (López-Gopar, 2016, p. 20). Zapotec is not part of the formal elementary and secondary schooling of the transborder students. In Oaxaca's recent history Zapotec has either been hidden as a point of shame or relegated to informal spaces in response to discriminatory ideologies. However, CETis 124, the high school in Tlacolula that the secondary students in this study attended, recently started a binational, intercultural program in collaboration with Haverford College in Pennsylvania. It is called Voces del Valle US-CETis 124 and is co-led by Drs. Felipe H. Lopez and Brook Danielle Lillehaugen. The program started in 2015 to create formalized educational spaces for Zapotec of the Tlacolula Valley, develop students' proficiency and pride in a language that is part of their home and community, and build connections across institutions (Lillehaugen, 2016, 2019; Vinculación DGETI Oaxaca, 2020). Since its inception, the collaboration has expanded to include the formal incorporation of some of Lopez's writings in course curriculum at CETis 124 (Lopez, 2018), as well as the use of Zapotec-centered pedagogical materials focusing on the history of Tlacolula Valley Zapotec. The work is reciprocal in nature, with CETis 124 students contributing to ongoing public scholarship, such as the revision of the open source teaching materials, including the chapters on the Zapotec number system (Flores-Marcial et al., forthcoming). This program is far from the norm for most Oaxacan high schools, but an exemplar of a way to uplift students' backgrounds and voices.

At the tertiary level, the largest public university in Oaxaca—UABJO—offers Indigenous language courses for students in the language education program. The program's stance to ensure that Indigenous languages are offered is aligned to its critical language education vision: Students are capable of responding to the educational needs of the Oaxacan community and of adapting to the different social and technological contexts of their state.

Español

FIGURE 5.4 A mototaxi awaits passengers in Tlacolula de Matamoros, Oaxaca.

We squeezed into the back of a mototaxi, essentially a three-wheeled golf-cart powered by the motor of a moped, going to Melchor's house. As we wind through the back dirt road in Tlacolula he tells the driver "por acá" and points to the left. I give Melchor a look meant to say "why didn't you just say left?" to which he responds, "I always forget words in Spanish."

> Se imagina el día que los deporten … y los mandan a México y cuando están aquí no hablan español. Qué van a hacer ellos?
> [Imagine if they get deported and they are sent back to Mexico and they don't speak Spanish. What are they going to do?]
> —*Antonio, Yauzin's father*

Historically, colonizers from Spain enforced the use of Spanish, thereby undermining and decimating Indigenous languages. Oaxaca is unique among other states in Mexico because Indigenous languages are still a part of many communities. Spanish, though, remains the language of power and formal institutions. Within the US, Spanish is the second most widely used language, with 13% of the population over the age of five speaking it (US Census Bureau, 2015). Spanish in the US is generally associated with Latinx populations, and it is often relegated to a lower status. However, this status shifts, depending on the speaker. When an immigrant from Mexico speaks Spanish or even if a Latinx US-born student learns Spanish, their language practices are devalued, especially if they don't also speak English. However, when a white student learns Spanish in a bilingual program they are praised (Valdés, 2018). This inequality was on display nationally during the US 2020 Democratic presidential primaries when Julián Castro, a US-born politician of Mexican origin, felt the need to justify his shortcomings in speaking Spanish while Pete Buttigieg, a white politician, was hailed for speaking Spanish (Agudo, 2019).

Uses of Spanish Within and Across Borders

For the transborder students in this study, Spanish was always the primary language spoken in their homes, and the language they relied on to communicate with their parents. Although the students talk about English being either their first language or the language they grew up speaking, Spanish was in fact the first language they learned at home. Students developed their linguistic repertoires and translanguaged using features of Spanish and English, a practice that is sometimes referred to as Spanglish (Otheguy & Stern, 2011). The children learned which features to use in which contexts: in Mexico, Spanish was the language of home, community, and schooling; in the US, the use of Spanish was limited to home and depending on where they lived, the community as well.

Once the transborder students started attending US schools, they began favoring English, and Spanish became a language in danger of being left behind. Yauzin's dad talks about the struggle to have his children continue speaking Spanish:

96 Issues Impacting Students

Ellos llegaban a la casa hablando en inglés y nosotros el español en la casa. Yo les decía a ellos que el español ellos lo iban a hablar porque ellos eran hispanos, porque ellos son nacidos en México, y ellos no son americanos pero también el español porque son sus raíces y no las vayan a dejar.

[They would come home from school speaking English and at home we speak Spanish. I told them they had to speak Spanish because they were Hispanic, they were born in Mexico, they were not Americans and I didn't want them to forget their roots.]

FIGURE 5.5 Yauzin, her brother, Tony, left, and younger cousin in Eutawville, South Carolina (2002).

To ensure that Yauzin and her brother stayed connected to their heritage, their mother Herminia spoke with them in Spanish and made a special effort to develop their literacy skills by having them write letters in Spanish to their family in Mexico. Both of Yauzin's parents encouraged their children to learn Spanish so they could maintain a strong connection with their country of origin. But there was also another reason, one related to their precarious undocumented status in the US:

Se imagina el día que los deporten, porque no es americano, porque han pasado muchas cosas que hay niñitos se van, no hablan español y los mandan a México cuando están aquí no hablan español y qué van a hacer ellos?

[Imagine if they get deported because they aren't American. They are sent back to Mexico and when they get here they don't speak Spanish, what will they do then?]

—Antonio, Yauzin's father

Undocumented families live with the daily pressure of being taken into custody and deported. Antonio feared that if his children stopped speaking Spanish and were forced to return to Mexico, they would stand out and be mistreated for being different from their peers. Unlike immigrants who have the security of legal permanent residency[2] or naturalized citizenship, undocumented families experience particular pressure to maintain their home languages.

When transborder students arrive in or return to Mexico—especially at the secondary and tertiary levels—they initially struggle with Spanish because they must use it in ways that differ from their US-based Spanish practices. Over time, though, they feel more confident:

Mi español cuando llegué fue no muy bien, fue un poco raro porque es como si fuera una americana hablando español que no podía pronunciar bien las palabras. Pero ahora que he estado aquí por tres años mi español ha mejorado mucho, igual al escribir.

[My Spanish was not very good when I arrived. It was like an American speaking Spanish who could not pronounce the words properly. But now that I have been here for three years, my Spanish has improved a lot and my writing too.]

—Sharely

Spanish in Schools

In the US most Mexican immigrant-origin students do not have access to bilingual education and therefore do not have opportunities for Spanish development in schools (Gándara & Hopkins, 2010). Furthermore, the growth of dual language bilingual programs has occurred within a context of gentrification where white, middle-upper class families often benefit more from these spaces than the immigrant-origin, minoritized students bilingual programs were originally intended to serve (Cervantes-Soon et al., 2017; Valdez et al., 2016). Only Melany had Spanish as part of her bilingual Pre-K program; everyone else was either in general education programs in English and/or English as a second or additional language programs that did not include Spanish in instruction.

For transborder students who found themselves suddenly learning in all-Spanish schools, writing posed the most difficulties. They had always spoke Spanish at home, but they did not typically read or write in that language. Fortunately, the closer alignment of the Spanish writing system with sounds (what many people refer to as the phonetic nature of the Spanish writing system, which is quite different from English) makes it easier to sound out words in Spanish and

98 Issues Impacting Students

subsequently read for meaning. The accent marks which are important to meaning-making in Spanish, and do not occur in English writing, caused difficulties for the students. Yauzin said she feared making writing errors when submitting papers in Spanish, which were required for courses such as educational psychology, linguistics, and writing. She worked through them, though, with the help of friends and by focusing on Spanish language structures within those university classes, even though it was not always taught explicitly.

Transborder students who sought to enroll at a university faced the highest stakes in terms of Spanish literacy. At the UABJO, even students who plan on studying English must take an entrance exam that tests content such as Mexican history, mathematics, and Spanish literature, entirely in Spanish:

> The first time I came for the exam I had problems with that. I remember looking at the questions, I didn't understand the questions. I knew how to do the problems, but there were words that I had never seen before ... I didn't pass the exam the first time. So the second time I got helped to get in.
>
> —*Erik*

Erik's experience with the college exam shows how the test is first and foremost an assessment of the language in which it is written, while the content is secondary (Menken, 2010). In spite of Erik's familiarity with the subject matter, his monolingual English schooling in the US rendered him unable to demonstrate his knowledge in Spanish. Using features of English through translanguaging was not permitted on the exam, even though he was applying to study English language education.[3] As a result, he had to look for a different approach to enter the university via connections and networks when he didn't score in the top 10% (for more on the public university admissions process see Chapter 6). Otherwise, Erik's difficulty reading and writing in Spanish would have barred him from being accepted to become an English teacher.

English

> I remember all my family in Mexico [saying] I didn't know how to speak Spanish because all my life I was talking English. Always in English.
>
> —*Brayan*

> No sé cómo aprendimos inglés, solo sé que nací y hablaba inglés.
> [I don't know how I learned English, I just know that I was born there and I spoke English.]
>
> —*Axianeydt*

Like Brayan and Axianeydt, most elementary and secondary transborder students in this study don't recall learning English. They have spoken it for as long as they can remember, often referring to it as their "first language" even though Spanish was the language they grew up with at home in Mexico and the US. English came into their lives once they entered US schools, and many became the most proficient English speakers in their families. Their parents, working long hours and caring for younger children at home, lacked the opportunity and time to learn a new language. As a result, the children served as cultural brokers (Orellana, 2009) who took on tasks such as translating or completing paperwork for their parents related to schools, taxes, medical visits, and even interactions with police in the case of an accident or of being pulled over. This was especially the case in states where English was the official language and access to documents translated into Spanish was limited.[4]

Views of English Within and Across Borders

"For adults who return from the US, culinary arts are the most valuable skills they bring back, but for children it's English," said a leader from the Instituto Oaxaqueño de Atención al Migrante (IOAM). Given the powerful position that English holds across the world, its speakers have access to a range of job opportunities. Transborder students and returned youth capitalize on their linguistic abilities, studying to become English teachers or finding employment in call centers where their English is valued and monetized (Anderson & Solis, 2014).

In alignment with the views of the IOAM leader who said that English was the most useful skill transborder students brought from the US, all three secondary students saw English as a key part of their economic future. This aligns with "the model of coloniality [whereby] the English language in Mexico and elsewhere is seen as *the* language to learn and *the* language of authority, economics and knowledge" (López-Gopar, 2016, p. 9). Brayan thought he might work as an English-speaking tour guide in Tlacolula, as a side job while he was in high school. "I'm thinking to work like a tour guide because in Sundays is like a flea market and lots of American people that speak English [come here] and I can help them, but they pay me," he explained. Melchor also saw English as a part of his future. "I want to study tourism because my English benefits me," he said. "I also want to know places and learn more cultures." He saw English as a way to connect with people from new places, and to reconnect him to people from the US, which he refers to as his "second home." Sharely was less certain about her future, but she did express a desire to become an English teacher. For all three secondary students, it was not just English, but their lived experiences in the US that shaped their career goals in Mexico, or even elsewhere.

One of the powers associated with English is its potential to be "the killer language," replacing the languages with which it comes into contact (Skutnabb-Kangas, 2003). Yauzin's dad saw this danger: "Pero ya como ellos empezaban a hablar el inglés, ya no quería hablar español" (When they started speaking English, they didn't want to speak Spanish anymore). Yauzin and her brother were not explicitly told about the hegemony of English, but learned it implicitly from

100 Issues Impacting Students

messages they received from schools, media, and society at large. The status of languages are lessons students in the US and elsewhere are taught via formal institutions, such as schools, as well as informal spaces that reinforce power structures and hierarchies. When students are brown, Spanish and/or Zapotec speakers, and immigrants from Mexico, the presence of white supremacy and xenophobia intensifies these lessons and heightens the pressure to assimilate.

Some transborder students in Mexico are proud of their English ability, while others are ashamed of it and disguise their proficiency (Bybee et al., 2021). Melchor's high school experience illustrates:

> I feel proud because it's [English] like a gift. It's also a disadvantage because that's the only thing they want me as a friend. I have two friends in my class who did not come from the US, but we talk in English. Sometimes in the class they start teasing us, they say "Ya deja el inglés, gringo." [Quit with the English, gringo]. I tell them "at least I have this thing and I'm proud of it."

López-Gopar and Sughrua (2014) found that speakers of English in Mexico are viewed as superior, but also "contested through the assertion of the subaltern knowledge that has been marginalized and discriminated against by coloniality" (p. 205). In Melchor's high school, English is associated negatively with being a gringo, a derogatory term used for people from English speaking countries, but also for Mexicans who have lived in the United States and may be more comfortable speaking English than Spanish. In Mexico, English speakers who don't have US connections are often products of bilingual private schools (Sayer & López-Gopar, 2015). It's rare for students in public schools to have access to the quality and quantity of English language education that their upper-class peers do (Despagne & Jacobo, 2016). Perhaps due to the reputation of English as an elite language, Melchor sees it as a gift that some of his public school peers have not received.

The elementary transborder students have limited access to English in Mexico because it's not part of their schooling. Karla and Axianeydt's primary opportunity to speak English is with their uncle, Diego, who lived in Oklahoma and now works as the coordinator of an English-language program in a private university in Oaxaca. But his long work hours don't allow for much time to practice English with his nieces. The girls choose not to flaunt their English among their peers in Mexico. Here the sisters describe Axianeydt's approaches:

INTERVIEWER: ¿A ti te gusta hablar inglés en la escuela? [Do you like to speak English in school?]

AXIANEYDT: No, porque me descubren todos. [No, because they'll discover I speak English.]

KARLA: A ella no le gusta cuando alguien sabe sobre su inglés. [She doesn't like when people find out she speaks English.]

INTERVIEWER: ¿Entonces ella quiere mantener en secreto que habla inglés? [So she wants to keep it a secret?]
KARLA: Ajá [Uh huh]
AXIANEYDT: Porque luego todos dicen, "¿Me enseñas inglés?" [Because then everyone would say, "Can you teach me English?"]

FIGURE 5.6 Karla, left, and Axianeydt, right, with their brother, Zayd, at the gate of their elementary school in Ciénaga de Zimatlán, Oaxaca (2015).

Beyond not wanting to help her peers, Axianeydt may also want to keep her English proficiency secret because she doesn't want to stand out, "show off," or be seen as different, even for a reason that can be perceived positively (Bybee et al., 2020, p. 136). Axianeydt's decision not to disclose her English practices may also emerge from a desire to shield the particulars of her migration experiences from peers, just as students from mixed-status families in the US are put in a position of disclosing or hiding their family's migration stories during formal instruction and informal conversations with peers (Mangual Figueroa, 2017).

At the higher education level it's also common for transborder students to withhold sharing about their US and English experiences (Hidalgo Aviles & Kasun, 2019). A professor of English education in Oaxaca said his students rarely volunteer that they have lived in the US. "Towards the end of the semester only one of them told me when I asked him directly," he said, "and he kind of shyly told me." Another professor believes students who hide their English skills do so because their peers "are envious of their English level and they themselves, the students who lived in the US, are sensitive about that."

102 Issues Impacting Students

English in Schools

Most public elementary schools in Mexico do not teach English, with a few exceptions of schools that bring in a circulating English teacher who moves between classes throughout the week. The elementary school in Ciénaga de Zimatlán did not offer English classes and the language was not visible anywhere in the school, in spite of the strong ties the community has to the US. However, after graduation Yauzin was employed through the Programa Nacional de Inglés (PRONI) to teach English in a Oaxacan public elementary school. The subject is not required in Mexico until secundaria, grades 7–9. Melchor describes the high school English classes as "really boring. It's not like in the US where English is really high; here you have to study ABCs, 123s, you have to translate what's a ball, tree, trash can, food." Sharely describes her role as an informal English tutor for her classmates:

> Being here in Oaxaca and having my English class is kind of boring because I already know all the things that my teachers show me. But my classmates, they barely know English, so it's difficult for them. So they treat me like good friends because I can help them. Sometimes they tell me, "what does this mean?" I don't give them the answers, but I tell them what it means so they can understand … I'm like a guide for them so they can understand more the class.

The tertiary transborder students were able to develop a more complex English repertoire in the US because they studied there through high school. As college students preparing to become English teachers—among peers who were much newer to English—they stood out. Ricardo said, "I feel that they see me as maybe an inspiration. It's a little funny when they see me standing up there in the podium talking or reading, but I don't feel superior to them." Along those lines, a professor in the language education program said, "I don't think they have a lot of problems integrating because of the huge currency they carry in their pocket, which is their English proficiency." Erik's college instructors not only took note of this, but leveraged his English to support his peers, and at the same time set him on the path to become a language teacher:

> I had two teachers that saw I knew a lot of English and asked me for help because in my class I think we were 45 students. The teachers that actually told me that I could help them around because the group was very big. I actually felt good for them to ask me because I can do something for them.

However, the positive recognition some transborder students receive for their English skills can at times be accompanied by criticism related to their understanding of the grammar of English. People who grow up speaking a language, but not studying its mechanics, may teach it differently than teachers trained in formal grammar. Yauzin reflects on her experience taking college classes to become an English teacher:

> When I arrived to Mexico and I started studying, I noticed my English was bad because I speak English the way people speak normally. But for a teacher, you have to know structure and grammar. For example, if you ask me how do you structure a simple sentence, I would be like "I don't know, I just know how to speak." But a teacher has to know those things and those things I learned here.

Although Yauzin characterized her English as "bad" upon her return to Mexico, she was actually referring to her knowledge *about* the language, what is often referred to as metalinguistic knowledge. As someone who spent eight years in the US speaking English and studying all the content areas in the language, she was able to easily communicate, read, and write in English. But because English instruction in the US teaches grammar in context or not at all (Weaver, 1996), she viewed her English as limited. While her linguistic knowledge of English was highly developed, she never had a reason to build up an understanding of the way English was structured, which was needed for her language education program.

Metalinguistic knowledge of a language is not required to successfully use it for communication (Gutiérrez, 2013). While such information may serve language teachers well, it is not critical knowledge for speakers of the language. For example, to say that they will have gone to the airport, a speaker does not need to know that they have used the future perfect tense. Unfortunately, transborder students are often judged by their command, or lack thereof, of this type of knowledge about English rather than how well they use it to communicate. This is partly because public school English programs developed at the federal level in Mexico are grammar-based. And teachers of the language "use the knowledge of grammar to tell the [transborder] kids, 'You may sound proficient, but let me tell you otherwise,'" explained a professor who prepares English teachers in Mexico. This judgment allows English teachers in Mexico who are less confident about their English practices to differentiate themselves from their transborder students.

Conversely, English teachers of transborder students in Mexico may feel inadequate or judged based on their position vis-à-vis a US-educated English-speaking student. One college English instructor said, "Yo sentía esa presión de que yo fuera a cometer errores o que no me supiera algo y eso sentía como que me iba a quitar autoridad en cierta forma" (I felt the pressure of making mistakes or not knowing something and that would seem as a lack of authority from me). Professor López-Gopar from the Facultad de Idiomas at the UABJO explained how this can happen within the Oaxacan context:

> Many of our [college] students are threatened because some of them may not have the supposed standard pronunciation of some words. They are corrected by those students who are retornados in their classes. They struggle basically to gain legitimacy just by ... being Oaxacan and most of them come from Indigenous backgrounds; most of our students are mestizos, in low socio-economic status so with that whole package of ... becoming the English teacher persona is questioned at different levels.

English in Mexican schools is a complex matter for transborder students and their educators, who may experience external judgement and/or internalized doubt in ways that can harm their sense of self and profession. While a language can open doors on a global scale, its speakers may not always want those doors to be opened, either for fear of being bullied about their English or for what it reveals about their migration history (Gallo, 2021; Despagne, 2019). But in spite of these perceptions, transborder students have found ways to leverage their English practices for their futures.

The Danger of Partial and Racialized Views of Transborder Students' Language Practices

Just as transborder students cannot be limited to a connection to just one country, the same is true for their language use. Translanguaging offers a more holistic and inclusive way to frame the linguistic realities of people who cross geographic and linguistic borders (García, 2009; García & Kleyn, 2016; Makalela, 2016). Translanguaging is the "use of language as a dynamic repertoire and not as a system with socially and politically defined boundaries that centers the unbounded language practices of multilinguals" (García & Li Wei, 2018, p. 1).

Translanguaging describes the linguistic practices of transborder students and families, as they language in their homes, schools, and communities within and between the US and Mexico. The notion of translanguaging recognizes each speaker's unique language system without regard to outside monitoring or the suppression of specific linguistic features in certain contexts (Otheguy et al., 2015). Yet it is often the opposite of what transborder students encounter, as they must grapple with external perspectives of language that bring forth stringent guidelines that restrict the use of specific linguistic features, particularly in schools and other institutions where people in power police the use of language.

The devaluation of the language practices of transborder students may take root for numerous reasons. First, the students are viewed through a monolingual lens that isolates the features of each named language and expects speakers to limit their language use within those boundaries. Second, because transborder students use language for different purposes across countries, they may develop their receptive abilities more than their productive abilities and may privilege oracy over literacy. As a result, their language acquisition may be viewed as incomplete

(Montrul & Silva-Corvalán, 2019). In fact, the transborder students are actually leveraging their linguistic repertoire purposefully based on the situations and people in each context. This is analogous to the literature on students labeled "long term English learners" in the US who have been problematically referred to as "lifers" for not being able to test out of the "English Language Learner" label; as "non-nons" for not being able to speak either language; or as semi-linguals due to a perception that their language systems are incomplete (Flores et al., 2015). Finally, in the US context, Mexican-origin immigrants are seen and heard from the white listening subject, "a perspective that privileges dominant white perspectives on the linguistic and cultural practices of racialized communities" (Rosa & Flores, 2017, p. 177).

The result is that their language practices—no matter how closely aligned to so-called standardized varieties—will always be seen as falling short due to their racialized identity (Rosa, 2019). However, from a holistic lens, transborder students have a full and constantly evolving linguistic repertoire that they draw on as they move across countries, states, cities, and towns.

Comparison Across Levels

In some spaces transborder students are free to translanguage, while in others they are confined to particular named languages and varieties of those languages. Their languaging experiences connect to how much time they have spent in each country, and in schools that mandate monolingualism in either English or Spanish. Pride, shame, and prestige play a role in how they view the features of their linguistic repertoire and consequently how they employ or suppress them in their everyday lives.

For the elementary students, being born in the US only led to English proficiency if they were able to attend school there. Otherwise, they primarily spoke Spanish at home and therefore did not experience much linguistic discomfort when they moved to Mexico where they continued speaking Spanish at home and eventually in school. With the lack of English instruction in public elementary schools and communities in Mexico, the young children had limited opportunities to speak and develop English. As a result, if or when they return to the US—which they can more easily do as US citizens—they will have to (re) learn English.

The secondary students' schooling experiences across countries was consistently absent of Zapotec, even though it was central to their families. Even though the students had varying features of English, Spanish and, for some, Zapotec in their repertoire, their schooling experiences in the US were completely in English, and they faced challenges learning in Mexico, as they had not had opportunities to develop the advanced Spanish literacy skills demanded by the classroom content they encountered there. The secondary students' experiences contrast with elementary transborder students, who study in English in the US, but benefit from

106 Issues Impacting Students

less challenging content classes where the basics of the Spanish language and literacy could get them through in Mexico. Secondary students struggled to make their Spanish work in the classroom, as well as outside of it with their peers. They experienced derogatory comments because of their US-influenced (estadounidense) Spanish. They were also teased for their fluency in English while alternatively or simultaneously sought after by their classmates for help in English classes. Despite these difficulties, they all saw English as a form of capital for their futures.

While the elementary and secondary students experienced ambivalence around their English proficiency, the tertiary students experienced more unambiguous positive recognition for their linguistic abilities, likely due in part to their enrollment in programs to become English teachers. Although students were excited to capitalize on their English abilities, they may have been restricted from entering other fields because the Spanish literacy requirements would have been too great given their English schooling in the US. Still, they worked to improve their Spanish writing. And like the secondary transborder students, they saw the potential to build upon their English from the US and capitalized on those skills by choosing to major in English education.

In the face of external and limiting views of transborder students that work to position them as incomplete, transborder students learn, unlearn, and relearn languages. It's common to hear "ni de aquí, ni de allá" (neither from here, nor from there), just as students may feel or hear they are not "American" enough in the US and not "Mexican" enough in Mexico. When it comes to their language practices, they may be positioned as inadequate, ni en inglés, ni en español, y tampoco en zapoteco (neither in English, nor in Spanish, and also not Zapotec). Yet, transborder students language in ways that allow them to adapt and thrive in their constantly changing linguistic landscape, as they develop and redevelop their sense of self and their connections to their families, communities, and countries.

Notes

1 Diidx zah is the variety of Zapotec from the San Pedro Quiatoni region of Oaxaca.
2 Legal permanent residents (LPRs) in the US can be deported, but it is not common. Reasons for deportation include: obtaining a green card through fraudulent means; conviction of certain crimes; abandonment of LPR status by residing outside of the US for one or more years.
3 In the US, teachers of Spanish or other languages also have to pass exams in English to be accepted into the university and become certified teachers.
4 While the US does not have an official language, 27 states have declared English to be their official language.

References

Agudo, R. (2019, July 27). There is nothing wrong with Julián Castro's Spanish. *The New York Times*. www.nytimes.com/2019/07/27/opinion/sunday/julian-castro-spanish.html.
Anderson, J., & Solis, N. (2014). *Los otros dreamers*. Independent Publication.

Bybee, E. R., Feinauer Whiting, E., Jensen, B., Savage, V., Baker, A., & Holdaway, E. (2020). "Estamos aquí pero no soy de aquí": American Mexican youth, belonging and schooling in rural, Central Mexico. *Anthropology & Education Quarterly*, 51(2), 123–145.

Bybee, E. R., Jensen, B., & Johnstun, K. (2021). Normalista perspectives on preparing Mexican teachers for American Mexican students. In P. Gándara & B. Jensen (Eds.), *The students we share: Preparing US and Mexican teachers for our transnational future* (pp. 71–96). SUNY Press.

Cervantes-Soon, C. G., Dorner, L., Palmer, D. K., Heiman, D., Schwerdtfeger, R. & Choi, J. (2017). Combating inequalities in two-way language immersion programs: New directions for bilingual education. *Review of Research in Education*, 41(1), 403–427.

Cruz-Manjarrez, A. (2013). *Zapotecs on the move: Cultural, social, and political processes in transnational perspective*. Rutgers University Press.

Despagne, C. (2019). "Language Is what makes everything easier": The awareness of semiotic resources of Mexican transnational students in Mexican schools. *International Multilingual Research Journal*, 13(1), 1–14.

Despagne, C., & Jacobo, M. (2016). Desafíos actuales de la escuela monolítica mexicana: el caso de los alumnos migrantes transnacionales. *Sinéctica*, 47.

Flores, N., Kleyn, T., & Menken, K. (2015). Looking holistically in a climate of partiality: Identities of students labeled 'long-term English language learners'. *Journal of Language, Identity & Education*, 14(2), 113–132. doi:10.1080/15348458.2015.1019787.

Flores-Marcial, X., García Guzmán, M., Lopez, F. H., Broadwell, Aaron., Plumn, M. H., Zarafonetis, M., & Lillehaugen, B. D. (forthcoming). *Caseidyneën saën—learning together: Colonial Valley Zapotec teaching materials*. Pressbooks. http://ds-wordpress.haverford.edu/ticha-resources/modules.

Gallo, S. (2021). Preparing educators for asset-based pedagogies: The case of recently-arrived transnational students in central Mexico. In P. Gándara & B. Jensen (Eds.), *The students we share: Preparing US and Mexican teachers for our transnational future* (pp. 119–144). SUNY Press.

Gándara, P., & Hopkins, M. (Eds.) (2010). *Forbidden language: English learners and restrictive language policies*. Teachers College Press.

García, O. (2009). *Bilingual education in the 21st century: A global perspective*. Wiley/Blackwell.

García O., & Kleyn, T. (Eds.). (2016) *Translanguaging with multilingual learners: Learning from classroom moments*. Routledge.

García, O. & Li Wei. (2018). Translanguaging. In C. Chapelle (Ed.), *The encyclopedia of applied linguistics*. Wiley. doi:10.1002/9781405198431.wbeal1488.

Gutiérrez, X. (2013). Metalinguistic knowledge, metalingual knowledge, and proficiency in L2 Spanish. *Language Awareness*, 22(2), 176–191.

Heidbrink, L. (2020). *Migranthood: Youth in a new era of deportation*. Stanford University Press.

Hidalgo Aviles, H., & Kasun, G.S. (2019). Imperial language educators in these times: Transnational voices from Mexico on nationalisms and returnee transnationals. *Educational Studies*, 55 (3), 262–270. doi:10.1080/00131946.2019.1570932.

Lillehaugen, B. D. (2016). Why write in a language that (almost) no one can read? Twitter and the development of written literature. *Language Documentation & Conservation*, 10, 356–393.

Lillehaugen, B. D. (2019). Tweeting in Zapotec: Social media as a tool for language activists. In J. C. Gómez Menjívar & G. E. Chacón (Eds.), *Indigenous interfaces: Spaces, technology, and social networks in Mexico and Central America*. University of Arizona Press.

Lopez, F. H. (2018). Liaza chaa "I'm going home". (Trans. B. D. Lillehaugen). *Latin American Literature Today*, 1(7). www.latinamericanliteraturetoday.org/en/2018/august/liaza-chaa-im-going-home-felipe-h-lopez.

108 Issues Impacting Students

López, L. E. (2006). Cultural diversity, multilingualism and indigenous education in Latin America. In T. Skutnabb-Kangas, O. García, & M. Torres-Guzmán (Eds.), *Imagining Multilingual Schools* (pp. 238–261). Multilingual Matters.

López-Gopar, M. E. (2016). *Decolonizing primary English language teaching*. Multilingual Matters.

López-Gopar, M. E., & Sughrua, W. (2014). Social class in English language education in Oaxaca, Mexico. *Journal of Language, Identity & Education*, 13(2), 104–110.

López Hernández, F. (2002). Lengua y migración. In Coordinación Estatal de Atención al Migrante Oaxaqueño (Ed.), *Memoria: Ciclo de conferencias sobre migración* (pp. 1–8). Gobierno Constitucional del Estado de Oaxaca.

Makalela, L. (2016). Ubuntu translanguaging: An alternative framework for complex multilingual encounters. *Southern African Linguistics and Applied Language Studies*, 34(3), 187–196.

Mangual Figueroa, A. (2017). Speech or silence: Undocumented students' decisions to reveal their citizenship status in school. *American Educational Research Journal*, 54(3), 485–523.

Menken, K. (2010). NCLB and English language learners: Challenges and consequences. *Theory Into Practice*, 49(2), 121–128. doi:10.1080/00405841003626619.

Mesinas, M., & Perez, W. (2016). Cultural involvement, Indigenous identity, and language: An exploratory study of Zapotec adolescents and their parents. *Hispanic Journal of Behavioral Sciences*, 38(4), 482–506.

Montrul, S., & Silva-Corvalán, C. (2019). The social context contributes to the incomplete acquisition of aspects of heritage languages. *Studies in Second Language Acquisition*, 41(2), 269–273.

Orellana, M. F. (2009). *Translating childhoods: Immigrant youth, language, and culture*. Rutgers University Press.

Otheguy, R., García, O., & Reid, W. (2015). Clarifying translanguaging and deconstructing named languages: A perspective from linguistics. *Applied Linguistics Review* 6(3), 281–307. doi:10.1515/applirev-2015-0014.

Otheguy, R., & Stern, N. (2011). On so-called Spanglish. *International Journal of Bilingualism*, 15(1), 85–100.

Perez, W., Vásquez, R., & Buriel, R. (2016). Zapotec, Mixtec, and Purepecha youth: Multilingualism and the marginalization of Indigenous immigrants in the United States. In H. S. Alim, J. R. Rickford, & A. F. Ball (Eds.), *Raciolinguistics: How language shapes our ideas about race* (pp. 255–272). Oxford University Press.

Rosa, J. (2019). *Looking like a language, sounding like a race: Raciolinguistic ideologies and the learning of Latinidad*. Oxford University Press.

Rosa, J., & Flores, N. (2017). Do you hear what I hear? Raciolinguistic ideologies and culturally sustaining pedagogies. In D. Paris & H. S. Alim (Eds.), *Culturally sustaining pedagogies: Teaching and learning for justice in a changing world*, (pp. 175–190). Teachers College Press.

Sánchez, G. K. (2018). Reaffirming Indigenous identity: Understanding experiences of stigmatization and marginalization among Mexican Indigenous college students. *Journal of Latinos and Education*. doi:10.1080/15348431.2018.1447484.

Sayer, P., & López-Gopar, M.E. (2015). Language education in Mexico. In W. E. Wright, S. Boun, & O. García (Eds.), *The handbook of bilingual and multilingual education* (pp. 578–591). John Wiley & Sons. doi:10.1002/9781118533406.ch37.

Skutnabb-Kangas, T. (2003). Linguistic diversity and biodiversity: The threat from killer languages. In C. Mair (Ed.), *The politics of English as a world language: New horizons in postcolonial cultural studies* (pp. 31–52). Brill.

Swain, M. (2006). Languaging, agency and collaboration in advanced second language proficiency. In H. Byrnes (Ed.), *Advanced language learning: The contribution of Halliday and Vygotsky* (pp. 95–108). Continuum.

US Census Bureau (2015). Detailed language spoken at home and ability to speakEnglish for the population 5 years and over: 2009–2013. www.census.gov/data/tables/2013/demo/2009-2013-lang-tables.html.

Valdés, G. (2018) Analyzing the curricularization of language in two-way immersion education: Restating two cautionary notes, *Bilingual Research Journal*, 41:4, 388–412, DOI: 10.1080/15235882.2018.1539886.

Valdez, V., Freire, J., & Delavan, M. (2016). The gentrification of dual language education. *The Urban Review*, 48 (4), 601–627.

Valdiviezo, L.A., Felis, M., & Browne, S. (2014). Language rights for social justice: The case of immigrant ethnolinguistic minorities and public education in the United States. In P. Orelus (Ed.), *Affirming language diversity in schools and society: Beyond linguistic apartheid* (pp. 147–164). Taylor & Francis.

Vásquez R. (2015). *La educación indígena de adolescentes en Oaxaca.* Unpublished report. Centro De Estudios Tecnológicos.

Vásquez, R. (2019). Zapotec identity as a matter of schooling. *Association of Mexican American Educators Journal*, 13(2), 66–90.

Velasco, P. (2014). The language and educational ideologies of Mixteco-Mexican mothers. *Journal of Latinos and Education*, 13(2), 85–106.

Vinculación DGETI Oaxaca (2020, December 1). Proyecto intercultural binacional Haverford College Pennsylvania, US-CETis 124 [Video]. YouTube. www.youtube.com/watch?app=desktop&fbclid=IwAR3Tjv7Q1_jtRISn3Cg-0oliDZgZRuV5Gvm Dvn7a7jiQnpVWAh-YYtpQrxg&feature=share&v=N4hlgDAKXdw.

Weaver, C. (1996). Teaching grammar in the context of writing. *The English Journal*, 85(7), 15–24.

6
TWO COUNTRIES, ONE EDUCATION

FIGURE 6.1 Yauzin with one of her elementary school students (2015).

My first motivation to come back was to continue
my studies and the second was racism.

—*Yauzin*

> This girl was really smart and I had a great connection with her. She used to come every morning and say, "Buenos días, maestra," and give me a chocolate or something. It was always something positive with her. A few months ago I bumped into her downtown. She's almost in high school now and she's doing great. She told me she is interested in learning English, so that made me very proud.
>
> *—Yauzin*

A common view of formal education is that its purpose is to prepare students for a career and improve their economic earning potential. This perspective fails to include the broader purpose of education, which is to position its students to participate fully in society on a national, transnational, and global scale (Hurn, 1993). Unfortunately, not all teachers and schools embrace this broader purpose and instead focus their teaching and learning experiences on the local or dominant culture, language, and history.

For many transborder students, schooling is the one constant as they migrate across borders. Yet school systems between nations and even within them vary drastically in policies and approaches toward transborder students. While some settings render invisible the unique experiences of these students, other spaces mandate programming focused on their language learning needs. Regardless of the approach, what persists across settings is the perception that the students' migration is behind them, when in fact movement between the US, Mexico, and beyond may continue to be a part of their lives. The result is that transborder students are often educated for a future that is misaligned with the reality of their migration cycles.

Most transborder students began their schooling in the US as immigrant-origin students—children born outside of the US or born to immigrants in the US—who were identified more by their language practices rather than their migration experiences (or those of their parents). Once in Mexico all the students continued their education and dealt with adjusting to learning in a less familiar country, culture, and language. This chapter compares the structures of schooling across countries, as well as the experiences of students and their educators in elementary, secondary, and tertiary schools in Mexico.

Elementary, Secondary, and Tertiary Educational Structures Across Countries

Public education systems in the US and Mexico differ significantly. There are additional variations across and within states, making adjusting to new schools challenging for both students and parents. Some of these differences are detailed below.

112 Issues Impacting Students

Centralized v. Decentralized Systems

The Mexican public education system is centralized nationally. The federalization was done under the guise of modernity "in order to teach Spanish and literacy to Indigenous peoples … to 'control' rural teachers" (López-Gopar, 2016, p. 37). Public schools throughout the country follow the same curriculum in grades 1–9 and use the same textbooks and workbooks. In contrast, US schooling is decentralized. Each state sets its own standards, and each local district implements those standards through different curricula and resources. In the US, there are greater opportunities to make education relevant to the local population; this is more challenging under Mexico's national curriculum. Each US state selects or creates standardized assessments for elementary and secondary students and the language(s) in which they are provided, although they are mostly in English. In Mexico, these assessments are in Spanish.

Compulsory Education

Schooling through high school is mandatory in both nations, though this has only been a requirement in Mexico since 2012. Until that point, schooling was only required through secundaria, or 9th grade. In the US, public school from Pre-K (depending on the state) or kindergarten through 12th grade is free. It is paid for by local tax dollars (i.e., state, city, district) and supplemented by federal funds. In Mexico schooling is free through secundaria or 9th grade, while at the bachillerato/prepa (high school) levels there is a matriculation fee. However, the reality is that schools at all levels require families to cover costs related to books, uniforms, supplies, school infrastructure, or curricular offerings such as computer classes (Martínez, 2019). These costs end up being just as high or higher than high school matriculation fees. This requirement acts as a barrier for students from low-income families. The average years of school completion in Oaxaca is 7.5. Nationally, only half of students in Mexico graduate from high school (INEE, 2018), compared to 75% of Latinx students in the US (Gándara & Contreras, 2009).

Melchor was surprised when he started high school, "I was like, why do I have to pay, I'm already used to not paying." This requirement undermines the mandatory schooling requirement because it is a barrier to families living in poverty. Sharely's family was teetering on the edge of not being able to afford her school's $37 US dollar matriculation fee per semester, which would have pushed her out of high school, in spite it being mandatory in the country.

School Days

The length of the school day differs significantly across countries. In Ciénega, Alberta would drop her three children at the elementary school at 8 a.m., return mid-morning to bring them a light meal, and pick them up at 12:30 p.m. She compared this with the US where, "you can drop your kids off at 7:00 a.m., they feed them breakfast and lunch and school gets out at 2:30 p.m." The 4.5 hour school day in Mexico—compared to about 7 hours per day in the US—leaves 3–4 hours for learning. Ezpeleta and Weiss (1996) found that instructional time in rural Oaxacan schools averaged 60–90 minutes per day. Most schools have a.m. and p.m. shifts, and many teachers work double shifts—sometimes in different schools—to make a livable wage. These punishing schedules and responsibilities make it difficult for teachers to find time for professional learning (Santibañez, 2021). Mexican secundarias and high schools increase class time by about 2 hours per day, bringing the total amount of learning time more in line with the typical US school day. In the US supplemental funding supports free breakfast, lunch, and after-school programs for students from low-income households. The absence of these programs places greater demands on families in Mexico with school-age children.

FIGURE 6.2 Alberta walks home Axianeydt after picking her up at primary school (2015).

School Closings (in Oaxaca)

There are more short- and long-term class cancellations in Oaxaca than in the US because of actions by the teachers' unions. While the overwhelming majority of public school teachers in the US and Mexico are union members, the teachers

114 Issues Impacting Students

union in Oaxaca is especially active. During the time of this study in 2014, the "Reforma Educativa" was newly enacted and the union was advocating for increased federal support of the education system and for the distribution of delayed payments to teachers. As a result, union activism frequently affected the day-to-day schooling of students. Melchor's mother explains the impact on her children's education:

> I prefer that my children attend school in the United States … because they attend school every day, and that's not the case here. [The teachers union has to take action] due to the government's lack of support. The teachers go on strike or organize marches. In fact, just last year one of my children was out of school for six months and that's when the grades started going down.
>
> —*Estefana, Melchor's mother*

Unions in the US are also very involved in issues of teacher compensation and educational reforms, but have less often relied on striking as a strategy. However, in 2018–2019 the US experienced a series of wildcat and union-led strikes in West Virginia, Oklahoma, Kentucky, and Arizona. Students missed anywhere from a day to several weeks of school as teachers stood up for a range of issues, including higher wages, smaller class sizes, and increased budgets for schools (Van Dam, 2019). In Oaxaca, strikes are much more common as teachers negotiate with political leaders to improve teaching conditions and the education of students who are Indigenous and from lower socio-economic statuses.

Student Composition

There are significant differences between the US and Mexican student composition. Racial, ethnic, and linguistic diversity—among other areas of social and human difference—are more prevalent in US schools given the nation's history of immigration from across the globe. Of all US students, 25% are immigrants (Camera, 2016), compared to 1% in Mexico (CEMABE, 2014). In the US transborder students are more likely to attend segregated schools with peers from minoritized backgrounds and lower socio-economic levels. They attend under-resourced schools in both countries, although the lack of resources between Mexico and the US is also uneven (Jensen, 2021). Sharely reflected on the differences between her peers after returning to Mexico:

> In Los Angeles everyone belongs to a group. For example, the popular kids, the geeks, the nerds, and so forth, whereas here you don't see that [in Oaxaca] … but in LA some are from Korea, some are from Mexico, some are from Africa. There are so many different cultures and those cultural differences create different groups. But here it's different, everyone is the same because we are all Mexican.

Herminia, Yauzin's mother, appreciated that her children encountered students from a range of backgrounds in South Carolina: "Y que los niños, conocieron, compartieron con morenos, blancos, hispanos de diferentes nacionalidades y eso fue lo bonito, eso me gusta mucho" (My children met Black, white, other Hispanics from different countries. That is something I liked the most). However, this is not to say that Mexican and especially Oaxacan public schools are lacking in diversity. While most students are of Mexican origin, some speak various Indigenous languages, may come from different parts of the country, or have transnational experiences living and learning in the US.

Admissions Policies and Practices

In the US, where most transborder students in this study began their schooling, the impact of immigration status on education differs between K-12 and college. The 1982 US Supreme Court ruled by a narrow 5–4 majority in the *Plyler v. Doe* case thereby requiring all students—regardless of immigration status—have access to a free and quality K-12 education. The students in this study were able to attend public schools through high school, but this uniform approach to education comes to a halt at the university level. Each state sets its own policies for college access and funding for undocumented students. This is why Yauzin, as noted in her opening quote for this chapter, decided to leave South Carolina, where her undocumented status barred her from being accepted to a public university.

Once in Mexico, many transborder students encounter immediate and significant challenges to school enrollment at all levels, even as Mexican citizens (Medina & Menjívar, 2015). For example, when educational documentation from the US is difficult to obtain, students may experience extended delays in their schooling as they attend to tedious bureaucratic requirements. However, efforts from groups such as Instituto para las Mujeres en la Migración (IMUMI) have advocated successfully to ease enrollment guidelines for US-educated students in Mexico. The government has loosened these processes at the elementary and secondary levels so that students can enroll in schools without an apostille (or apostillado in Spanish), an international certificate of authenticity, as per Mexico's Acuerdo Secretarial (Government Agreement) 286 of 2015.

However, the apostille is still a requirement for US-educated students who study in Mexican universities. For Yauzin, the college enrollment process was a multifaceted one:

> Before the whole college process, I had to do a different set of paperwork with the Secretaría de Educación Pública (SEP) de Oaxaca. First, I was told to go to the SEP to revalidate my classes from high school. They told me I needed an "apostillado," which is a document given by the Office of the Secretary of State, that certifies my studies in the US. However ... I had to

116 Issues Impacting Students

be in the USA to get the document. I was already here and the only ones who could help me were my parents, because they were still in South Carolina, and my guidance counselor. I got in touch with my counselor many times but she just didn't seem to have the time or patience to help me … Once she finally did it, she sent me the wrong document … the paper she sent me was just a copy and I needed [an original] to get the real apostille.

So this time I let my parents take care of the situation. I was afraid because none of them spoke English, luckily my little brother was there to help them translate. My parents went to my high school, talked to the guidance counselor and asked her for my transcript. Once they had that in their hands, they headed for Columbia, South Carolina, to the Office of the Secretary of State. My parents were lucky to find someone who spoke a little Spanish … I guess they felt pity for my parents because they were able to do all the paperwork there and then without my presence. [They paid] $2 USD for the apostille, they were very pleased when they saw the golden seal on the document, which meant it was the real deal.

After I had the document in my hands, I was able to go back to the SEP with the apostille, my high school transcript and report cards from middle school. I was shocked when they asked me for the report cards because I was always told they weren't important, just the transcript. Luckily, I always kept them as if I knew I would need them again. For the middle school revalidation, I didn't need an apostille, my report cards were enough … I remember having to pay around 500 pesos for the translation of all my documents. The SEP sent me to [a private college] to translate my documents, so I went there. The whole process took me around 2–3 months because of all the problems I went through; not having the apostille, and also because of all the strikes and closings of the SEP by teachers, parents from different towns of Oaxaca and many puentes [holidays].

After all that chaos, I went to the UABJO to start my college process and when the secretary saw that my documents were different from the rest of the other students, she asked me to explain what that was. I told her everything and she told me I had to get a letter of recommendation from the president of my municipio. At that time, I lived in San Bartolo Coyotepec and I had just moved there so nobody knew me, not even the president. I was so scared and sad because I didn't know what to do. Luckily for me, my aunt's husband was well known around the town and the president knew him… I explained to him my situation and I told him I knew he didn't know me, but that I was a good and honest person and I wanted to continue my studies. When I told him I was Horacio's niece everything changed. He said "Just because I know Horacio I will give you the letter of recommendation." At that moment I didn't care about anything else, I was glad I got it. It was a really bad experience and moment of my life, but thankfully, I got everything in order and I was able to go to college and graduate from the languages department.

Yauzin's roller coaster experience to obtain the apostille she needed to certify her US high school diploma for college in Mexico—as a Mexican citizen—shows why higher education may be out of reach for US educated transborder students. Not only did this process require Yauzin to overcome an array of bureaucratic obstacles, but she also had to rely on her personal connections in the US and Mexico. Fortunately, unlike some transborder students who return to Mexico with their families, she benefited from her parents and brother being in the US because they were able to collect and validate the required documents. But even the US documents were not enough. She had the additional hurdle of obtaining a letter of good character from her town's president. Once again, she was fortunate to have a family connection. Had that not been the case, her dreams to complete college could have been thwarted in Mexico, just as they were in the US.

Higher Education Systems

Undergraduate education differs greatly between the US and Mexico. In the US, students take general education classes that span humanities, history, math, sciences, and languages, for example, prior to more specialized coursework in their major. In Mexico, students only take coursework in their major for their undergraduate degrees. But regardless of the different approaches, transborder students in both nations face access challenges. Statistics on US educated students in Mexican colleges are not readily available. But in the US only 5–10% of undocumented students attend college, compared to approximately 50% of their 18- to 21-year-old documented peers (US Department of Education, 2015). Higher education for transborder students is often the exception, despite their preparation, motivation, and long-term goals.

Presence and Absence of Language Learning Programs and Services

Whether transborder students receive an equitable education across borders depends greatly on each country's history with migration and the presence or absence of policies that provide transborder students rights beyond those afforded to their peers who are not learning in a new language, culture, or nation. The *Lau v. Nichols* (1974) US Supreme Court case determined that students who were new to English or developing their proficiency had a right to supplemental language education. Consequently, US public schools were required to offer additional programs to create equitable learning opportunities for multilingual students. Unfortunately, implementation, funding and quality of these programs differs from state to state and district to district.

Mexico does not have a related policy for students from English-speaking backgrounds—either new arrivals or returnees—who must adapt to learning in Spanish. However, the 2003 *General Law of the Linguist Rights of Indigenous Peoples*

118 Issues Impacting Students

acknowledges the importance of culturally and linguistically relevant education. Nonetheless, it stops short of requiring specific policies, instead stating that, "access to bilingual and intercultural education is granted, and in secondary and tertiary (university) education, interculturalism, multilingualism and the respect for diversity and linguistic rights will be promoted" (Hamel, 2008, p. 308). This law is neither widely known nor regularly enforced (N. Martinez Miguel, personal communication, November 20, 2020).

Bilingual Education and TESOL Programs in the US

In school districts across the US, educators are generally accustomed to working with immigrant-origin students. Teachers who specialize in bilingual education and teaching English to speakers of other languages (TESOL) are prepared to work with this subgroup. However, teachers certified in other areas also have emergent bilingual students in their classrooms but may feel unprepared to educate them in ways that are inclusive of their full cultural and linguistic repertoires (Gomez & Diarrassouba, 2014; Schissel & Reyes, 2020).

School systems give the bureaucratic label of "English Language Learner" to students identified as requiring additional support to learn English. These students must receive English or bilingual language services as per *Lau v. Nichols*. Few of them, however, have access to schools with Spanish-English bilingual programs. Even for those who do have access to these programs, Spanish might be a new language if students come from Indigenous families who speak a language such as Zapotec or Mixtec at home. Further, these minoritized languages can become a source of shame that they do not readily admit to knowing in educational spaces (López-Gopar, 2014).

In general, TESOL programs are much more readily available than Spanish-English bilingual programs. Among the nine transborder students in this study, only Melany had one year of bilingual education (as a Pre-K student); the rest were all part of TESOL (or ESL) programs. English was thus their primary learning language; their Spanish and Zapotec were not leveraged as educational strengths. Students were denied support in their home language and the opportunity to develop Spanish and/or Zapotec oracy and literacy in school.

In spite of the English focus of TESOL programs, educators can take a stance to make space for students' multilingual practices within their classrooms (Kleyn & García, 2019; Tian et al., 2020). ESL settings can also be a place for students to connect with peers who have had similar migration and linguistic backgrounds. Erik and Yauzin's experiences varied based on the languaging practices of their teachers and peers:

> They put me with a teacher that had experience with other ESL students, but she didn't speak any Spanish so that made it hard and every time we had to do an assignment. She always told the classmates to write something for me.
>
> —*Yauzin*

I started at the ESL program and that's where I met a lot of my friends. Then, I started making new friends. My first teacher spoke Spanish and English, that kind of helped me out too and later on I started learning English ... I got out of the program four years later when I had finished 10th grade because they saw that I had improved a lot and I wouldn't have any problems.

—*Erik*

Yauzin refers to a teacher who has "experience with ESL kids," even though ESL is a program and not a label for students (Kleyn & Stern, 2018). Her comment highlights the fact that many students in ESL programs are only with a designated ESL teacher for part of the school day. The rest of the time they are with educators who are prepared to teach a content area or grade level but do not know how to best support students who are learning in a new language. This can result in problematic practices, such as Yauzin's teacher asking her classmates to do her work for her. Conversely, Erik had an ESL teacher who was able to communicate with him in Spanish as well as English, which likely supported his language development. He was able to connect with peers who were also language learners before branching out to those outside of the ESL program.

While some TESOL programs may create spaces for students' home language practices, as in the case of Erik, many fall short of providing students with the Spanish that will prepare them for learning in Mexican schools. Bilingual programs, on the other hand, create spaces for students to develop both languages simultaneously because they are learning content while becoming biliterate. These programs are better aligned with the realities of transborder students who experience schooling in at least two languages. That said, bilingual programs still fall short of creating spaces for the Indigenous languages that are part of the linguistic repertoire of some Mexican-origin students.

While the quality of bilingual and TESOL programs across the US varies, their mandatory availability is a starting point to improve the education of students who are becoming multilingual and multicultural. Due to Mexico's out-migration history, the public education system lacks sufficient structures and programs to support the language learning of US-educated transborder students.

Public School Language Support Programs and Resources in Mexico

The limited availability of bilingual education in the US to immigrant-origin students results in many transborder students arriving in Mexican schools with a monolingual English education. Mexican schools struggle to support Spanish development in transborder students because they are more accustomed to sending students to the US rather than receiving students who have been educated there. Public schools do not offer programs similar to TESOL in the US, and bilingual Spanish-English education is limited to private schools, whose students

120 Issues Impacting Students

come from families with greater economic resources (Sayer & López-Gopar, 2016). Meanwhile, secondary transborder students sit through English classes geared toward students new to the language. They grow bored and frustrated. Worse, their English practices diminish because of limited opportunities to speak, read, and write in the language.

In the absence of programming that would provide Spanish support to transborder students, there are small scale programs being developed in Mexico and between Mexico and the US to support students and prepare teachers for this growing subgroup. Community organizations in Zacatecas and Sonora have implemented a program to provide US-based textbooks to transborder students so that they can continue learning content as they learn Spanish (Délano Alonso, 2018). In spite of a limited school-based educational approach, the Mexican government has acknowledged this group of students and has created materials focused on the experiences of transborder students.

La Secretaría de Educación Pública (SEP), the Mexican department of public education, developed a series called "Aquí y Allá" (Here and There). It included the seminal book for educators and policy makers by Zúñiga, Hamann, and Sánchez García (2008), *Alumnos transnacionales: las escuelas mexicanas frente a la globalización* (*Transnational students: Mexican schools in the face of globalization*), to outline the key concepts, data, and recommendations for a subgroup that had received very little attention at this time. SEP also published a bilingual Spanish–English workbook called, *Mientras llego a mi escuela/While I get to school* (Secretaría de Educación Pública, 2008), geared toward students in Mexico with experiences in US schools. It includes activities ranging from students writing their own migration stories and tracing them onto a map of North America to charts that translate grading scales between the US and Mexico to matching key holidays with corresponding symbols from each country. The workbook ends with information for parents and families about their children's educational rights in Mexico.

Binational Teacher Education Programs

The lack of programs and preparation of educators to support transborder students—in Mexico and the US—is in part due to the mononational approach to teacher education, even in the areas of bilingual education or TESOL. To reverse this approach, a program called Formadores de Docentes Binacionales (FDB) (Binational-Bilingual Teacher Education) has been piloted as a collaboration between the Secretary of Public Education in Baja California, Mexico, and universities, the education department, and the organization for bilingual education in the state of California. FDB works with educators in both countries on curriculum modules that:

1. develop critical consciousness related to the sociopolitical, sociocultural, sociolinguistic, and social-emotional dimensions of binational education;
2. understand how these dimensions shape students' educational experiences;

Two Countries, One Education   **121**

3. advance their pedagogical approaches to build on binational students' assets and academic challenges; and
4. develop a sense of agency and advocacy for the education and well-being of immigrant students and their families (Alfaro & Gándara, 2021, p. 62).

Although FDB is a pilot program, it is a promising approach that is rooted in binational collaboration that is two-way at its core. It also centers the experiences of transborder students and normalizes migration. It's an example of new directions in teacher education and programs for students that move beyond mononational and monolingual frames.

Views and Experiences of Teachers and Teacher Educators in Mexico

Educators in Mexico speak about their frustration of not being prepared to teach transborder students (Bybee et al., 2021; Román González & Sánchez García, 2021). The elementary and secondary teachers interviewed for this study did not learn about transborder students in their teacher education program, nor did they receive related professional development in their schools. An elementary school teacher acknowledges that "es nuestra realidad y tenemos que conocer para poder atender a esos niños porque los estamos ignorando" (it is our reality and we have to be familiar with them in order to assist these kids because we are ignoring them). Transborder students arrive needing to learn the customs (such as flag ceremonies), behavioral expectations, and pedagogical approaches of Mexican schools, as well the fundamentals of Spanish literacy. Without an identification process, schools overlook or ignore these needs, and transborder students disappear into the general population.

Educators need support in addressing these areas. Higher education faculty members who prepare teachers are becoming aware of this gap in their programs:

> To be honest, in our program we are doing zip as to talking about these issues with our student teachers. What is it that we do when we have those students who come from the States? How do we profit from the English levels that they bring? Do we make them feel good in their English classes? Because many of them I think especially in elementary school, but more importantly in middle and high school when there are teenagers, fitting in is a huge thing for them and many times many of them basically don't tell anybody that they speak English.
>
> —*Professor López-Gopar, UABJO*

Asking these questions about the coursework of future teachers is an important first step in ensuring that transborder students receive an education that is inclusive of their backgrounds and needs. An elementary school teacher said, "No nos

122 Issues Impacting Students

dice que trabajemos con estos niños que vienen de Estados Unidos, simplemente nos dice que no los separemos, que trabajemos igual" (They don't tell us how to work with these kids who come from the US, they only tell us not to segregate them and work with them the same way as the other students). This connects to the principle in *Lau v. Nichols* that equal opportunities do not guarantee equitable outcomes for students with different needs. Applied in a Mexican context, the principle is a reminder that educating all students without taking into account migratory, cultural, and linguistic backgrounds leads to unequal outcomes.

When asked about what, if any, adjustments are being made to educate transborder students in Mexico, some teachers spoke about sending these students to work with special education teachers (Bybee et al., 2021). An elementary school teacher responded to how transborder students factor into the larger population served by the special education teacher: "no nada más alumnos que tengan ese problema, también trabaja con alumnos que tengan una discapacidad, problemas de lenguaje, hay una maestra de educación especial y ahí van varios de diferentes clases, ahí se juntan" (not just with them, she also works with students with disabilities, speech problems. The special education teacher works with all those students).

While this approach acknowledges needs of US-born or -raised students, it conflates transborder students who are learning or developing a language for a new purpose (i.e., schooling) with those who have been labeled with a disability. It pathologizes students based on their geographical, cultural, or languaging circumstances. This phenomenon parallels the overrepresentation of emergent bilingual students in special education in the US (Cioè-Peña, 2020). In the absence of specialized services that focus on Spanish development for transborder students in Mexico, this approach may be viewed as "better than nothing." However, it also sends a strong negative message about the language practices of transborder students.

Another elementary school teacher thought it would be useful for educators to be able to communicate in English with their transborder students. He said, "Pues que tuviéramos una clase inglés para los maestros para que si pudiéramos comunicarnos con ellos" (We should have English classes for teachers so we could communicate with these students). This approach would certainly help students and educators understand one another better and would also give teachers a better basis from which to teach different languages. That said, it still does not address the socio-political understandings and pedagogical techniques required to teach transborder students.

A 3rd grade teacher who acknowledged her insufficient preparation to teach transborder students nevertheless takes steps to include their realities in her instruction:

> La semana pasada hablamos de la migración, lo que es y en qué consiste. Vimos todo lo que pasaba, en qué consistía, por qué iban sus familias, para buscar condiciones de vida. Qué problemas enfrentaban y cosas así. A mí me gusta que expresen sus ideas, sentimiento y emociones porque ellos son niños y tienen mucho de qué hablar.

[Last week we talked about immigration. What it is and it means. We talked about its implications, why families migrate, living conditions, the problems they face among other things. I like that they express their ideas, feelings and emotions because they are kids and have many things to say.]

Including the lived experiences of transborder students in the classroom, and in this case the factors that cause families to migrate, makes them visible and positions students as experts. Although the focus of this lesson was migrating from Mexico, rather than returning from the US to Mexico, it is a starting point that can be built upon in future lessons. It is also a way to build empathy and understanding among students, which could help reduce the tendency of Mexican students to tease their transborder classmates.

At the college level, a professor saw that transborder students had the potential to support the English learning of their peers. He explained, "I had them informally give tutorials to the other students. They seemed to like it and that helped me a lot … [I noticed] they tended to take more pride in their academic level." The importance of this approach is to simultaneously include spaces for reciprocity in which all students have the opportunity to serve both as experts and learners rather than being permanently relegated to one or the other.

Schooling Experiences Between the US and Mexico

FIGURE 6.3 Axianeydt, left, marches with the honor guard during the ceremony for her graduation from 6th grade (2017).

124 Issues Impacting Students

What stands out for transborder students in their transnational schooling experiences are not so much macro structures, but micro moments. Most of the students started their formal education in the US and used that as their point of reference when they arrived in or returned to Mexico. Brayan reflects on his time in the US schools as "perfect" because of the freedom he had there compared to the stricter guidelines in Mexican schools:

> I liked that in school I don't have to wear uniform. They don't order me to cut my hair, you can have it as long as you wanted. We had birthday parties in there and I liked all my life when I lived there because it's so perfect, it's so beautiful that place.

In the US, students usually only wear uniforms in private schools, with the exception of major metropolitan areas like New York City. While US public schools have dress codes, as Brayan notes, students are generally free to wear and style their hair as they like (although some schools have tried to regulate the hair of Black students, particularly with Afro-centric hairstyles). Mexico, by contrast, requires uniforms in public schools and mandates that boys wear their hair short to adhere to conservative gender norms. While Brayan spoke about his US life as "so perfect" and "beautiful," he was not able to elaborate on what exactly he meant. He may also have been referring to a particularly contented time in his childhood, as his view comes across as somewhat idealized.

Karla and Axianeydt—whose schooling has primarily been in Mexico—have strong preferences. They spoke about the delicious pepperoni pizza sold at the school cafeteria, but expressed less enthusiasm about their teachers. Axianeydt said "nos jalaban las orejas y tiraban nuestros lápices al piso. Cuando nos va mal en una materia nos dicen que no quieren niños flojos, pero cuando no nos dan trabajo, no hacemos nada" (They pull our ears and they throw our pencils on the floor. When we are not doing well in a subject they say that they don't want any lazy kids there, but when they don't assign a task we don't have anything to work on). In terms of the type and amount of work, Ricardo noticed a significant contrast between US and Mexican high schools, both of which he attended during his senior year:

> There was a big difference. In the USA my senior year I had a literature teacher and he was very open. We had to read a lot of books and [took] written exams. Here, if you want to you can read, [but] you copy paste most of your homework. They are a little more laid back, the assignments were less in quantity. I mean here they maybe give you 10 problems in mathematics, over there we had to do 30.

Beyond these academic differences, Tere, Sharely's mom, noticed the way parents and children connected to one another differed between the two countries.

Sharely picked up on these norms too and was quick to request that her mother change her behavior. Tere said:

Allá en Los Ángeles yo la iba a dejar y también a traer. Entonces yo fui a traerla y me pregunto que por que había ido y yo le dije que fui a traerla. Al tercer día me dijo que ya no la fuera a traer porque nadie va a recoger a sus hijos. Nosotros estábamos acostumbrados a saludarnos de beso y después me decía que ya no me iba a dar beso frente a sus compañeras.

[In Los Angeles I went to drop her off and pick her up. ... On the third day she told me not to pick her up anymore because nobody comes to pick up children. We were used to greeting each other with a kiss but later she said she was not going to give me a kiss in front of her friends.]

FIGURE 6.4 Sharely, left, and Nancy, reading on the bed they share in their home in San Juan Guelavía, Oaxaca (2017).

The public warmth and affection between family members differs across cultures, and Sharely clearly wanted to fit in just like many students do. A parent's visibility in their child's schooling—such as dropping them off and picking them up—is something students notice in terms of how they compare with their peers. This is not something unique to transborder students, but it does bring in an additional layer of cultural difference that has to be negotiated across national contexts.

Advocacy Amid Adjustment

Schools in the US and Mexico generally do not center the experiences and needs of transborder students. US schools have programs to support students with language learning, but they are often peripheral to the general education population. Mexican schools have no supporting policies or programs, and transborder students are not generally on the radar of educators. As a result, students and their families must advocate for themselves when the system overlooks them.

When Yauzin started attending a public middle school in South Carolina, she was the only Latina and the only Spanish speaker in her class. She felt stressed and isolated, and her family had to intervene:

> I was being kind of mistreated by my classmates and I was crying all the time at home and at school. I was like "I want to go back to Mexico, I don't want to be here, I don't want to go to school anymore." So they decided to go and talk to the principal and at that time my uncle was married to an American lady so she did us the favor of translating. After they talked to the principal and the members of the school, they changed me to another 6th grade class where there was a Hispanic girl. She was born in the States, but her parents are from Guatemala so they put me in her class so she could help me and translate and explain what was going on in the lesson.
>
> —*Yauzin*

Supported by her family and an English speaking in-law, Yauzin was able to move into a setting in which she was not the only Spanish speaker. However, other immigrant families may hesitate to make demands about their children's education. They care for their children, but they may also feel that teachers are the experts and they should not tell them what to do (Carreón et al., 2005). Furthermore, school structures are often set up to encourage families to play a role in activities such as volunteering and fundraising, but they are discouraged from participating in curriculum decisions, program development, and student placement (Ramirez, 2003). Finally, undocumented families may feel intimidated or frightened by the idea of entering into a public school building, a space of authority, so they stay out of schools despite wanting to advocate for a better education for their children (Mangual Figueroa, 2013; Turner & Mangual Figueroa, 2019).

Transborder students who resume their schooling in Oaxaca may also require external advocacy to get the support they need following a mostly English, monolingual education in the US. Melchor explains how he had to stand up for himself to explain his migratory experiences:

> None of them [the teachers] knew until I told them, "I am not really good because I came from the US. Just speak slower or give me extra classes."

Then they were more helpful. First they just looked at me and said, "How could you come from the US, you look like a normal Mexican that speaks Spanish?" ... After I told them [my experience] they saw me in a different way.

Being of Mexican-origin allows transborder students who are (back) in the country to fit in more than immigrants in the US who may attend schools where the majority of the student body is of a different racial or ethnic group (as Yauzin experienced in South Carolina in a school with mostly US-born Black students). However, when students like Melchor blend in within Mexican schools, educators may overlook their differences and needs at the expense of their learning. Melchor spoke up for himself to ensure he would have the supports needed to learn in Spanish.

Sharely had a similar experience in Mexico that related to her challenges with Spanish literacy:

> Coming back to Oaxaca and starting a new school was difficult because I had to learn and write Spanish ... I was like nervous because I didn't really know how to do that. The teachers got a bit mad, but my mom talked to them and they understood that I didn't know much Spanish so that helped me a lot.

FIGURE 6.5 Sharely talks with the teacher in her 10th grade computer class at the CETis 124 high school in Tlacolula de Matamoros, Oaxaca (2015).

128 Issues Impacting Students

In cases of Sharely and Melchor, they may have been viewed as incapable when in fact they were simply new to learning in Spanish. Their US schooling in English did not prepare them for Mexican schooling in Spanish. Additionally, their Mexican origin made them invisible to educators unaccustomed to asking students about their educational and migration backgrounds, information necessary to better support them in school (Bybee et al., 2021; Zúñiga et al., 2008). Advocacy from the students and families was required to ensure they got an education responsive to their academic, linguistic, and socio-emotional needs.

College Entry and Major Selections

> We only know the successful stories that made it, not the ones that did not make it or did not have the connections to get into college.
>
> —*Professor López-Gopar*

Higher education is often out of reach for transborder students in the US and Mexico. State policies limit opportunities for undocumented students in the US. They may be banned from attending public institutions altogether, required to pay out-of-state tuition that is double or triple in-state rates, or denied public scholarships and financial aid. In Mexico, where one-quarter of the college-age population is able to enroll in higher education, transborder students face additional challenges, even as citizens (Cortez Román & Hamann, 2014). Documentation to validate their US schooling can be a major hurdle, as Yauzin's example illustrates. Moreover, US-educated students must compete for limited public university spots. For example, the UABJO, to which many transborder students apply, accepts only about 30% of the 600–700 applicants who apply each year. Professor López-Gopar describes the process of the Spanish exam:

> The test includes facts about Mexican history that I don't even remember. The stupid stuff that you can think of that has no connection whatsoever with our BA, but they have to take it. Those who score in the top would have to have attended a very strong high school or be a very good high school student.
>
> Then there's a huge political process where those who didn't take the exam or failed try to get in. Many times we have a second exam, but it's basically more about connections from having a strong person in the university who can maybe talk to the director of the facultad that recommends you or a high up political favor, like maybe the uncle knows someone who is a senator. And that is also financial because many spots are even sold.
>
> So in those cases of retornados ... they are at a disadvantage because the test is in Spanish and it's usually done under the table and they don't have the connections and they struggle just to get into college.

Transborder students face significant obstacles to higher education on both sides of the border. In Mexico they face a Spanish admission exam that is dependent on limited and localized knowledge, the lack of political or university connections, and costly fees. In the US, they must overcome restrictive, prohibitive, or costly policies that limit access and funding. Yauzin lived in South Carolina, where policies blocked access to public college for undocumented students.[1] She was successful in high school and local colleges sought her out. "I received many applications from different universities," she said, "but I was like, 'No thank you, I can't' [the law won't permit me]." Yauzin's decision to return to Mexico was solidified by her desire to continue her studies after high school and aligns with Cortez Román & Hamann's (2014) finding that undocumented high school graduates in the US who cannot attend college in the country view returning to Mexico as an avenue to reach their higher education and career goals.

Once students apply to a university in Mexico, they must immediately select a major. English education is a popular major for transborder students because in the US most studied exclusively in English (Cortez Román & Hamann, 2014). This choice can be both beneficial and harmful. On the one hand, English education gives them a strong background in oracy and literacy; on the other, it deprives them from developing Spanish for school and, subsequently, work. All other majors are taught fully in Spanish, a deterrent for some students even when the content is more aligned to their interests. One professor in the school of language education narrated how transborder students may think through their decision: "'Well, I may lack Mexican History ... I may lack strong academic Spanish skills. However I have English.' So I think the Facultad de Idiomas is certainly a big attraction for them."

Asked how living in the US affected her decision to study English education, Yauzin credited her professional aspiration to her time spent in the US:

> Probablemente no, probablemente hubiera estudiado something related to marine biology. I wanted to be a marine biologist so bad and I also like the sea very much. But I don't think I would have studied English as a major if I didn't live in the states.

Yauzin was raised in the southern part of Oaxaca by the Pacific Ocean, and her interests were tied to her Mexican environment. Migrating to the US changed her plans, just as it did for the other transborder students who also selected the English language teaching pathway (Cortez Román & Hamann, 2014).

For Ricardo studying English was a default when at age 18 he had to make a decision about his future. "I sort of decided here," he said. "When I was in high school, I didn't have any goals so I was like 'what am I gonna do now?' It was at random, I just chose it." He did not have a passion for studying language education, but neither was the choice entirely "random." Ricardo went on to say, "I want to finish my studies and get a job as an English teacher ... I suck at Spanish." His perception of his Spanish and the reality of having to study college-level content in Spanish likely deterred him from selecting another major, one he might have pursued had he remained in the US.

There have been efforts to reduce the shortage of English teachers in Mexico by building on the strengths of US-educated people in Mexico. One example is a primarily online program that is a collaboration between the University of Dayton Publishing, La Fundación SM México, and Otros Dreams en Acción (ODA), an organization based in Mexico that supports young deportees or returnees. ODA advertised the program on its Facebook page as follows:

> Teaching English may not have been "your dream" before deportation/return, heck, it may not be your dream while living in exile from home and familia in the United States either! But it IS a viable option for income and community, and there IS high demand. Teaching English has become a stepping stone to realizing sueños (for example, supporting family, travelling around the world, going to college, or making a film) for many who have come before you.
>
> —*Otros Dreams en Acción, 2017*

As this post shows, English teaching in Mexico is an opportunity for US returnees, albeit one that may be more circumstantial than one rooted in the goals people may have had prior to being back in Mexico.

Transborder Students Becoming English Language Teachers

FIGURE 6.6 Yauzin teaching English to a class of primary school children (2015).

> Those students were challenging for me. They were very energetic. They were talking all the time and they used to frustrate me a lot. In the end, they were very nice, but it was hard to work with them. They were not as interested in learning English as they were in getting to know me. Their [general education] teacher and I had a good connection, though. She gave me a lot of freedom to work with the students [as their English teacher].
>
> *—Yauzin*

The 30% of applicants who are accepted into the Facultad de Idiomas all have widely different English abilities, which are not measured as part of the entry exam or any other admissions process:

> In our program by principle we don't require a level of English. We accept students with any level of English because of the socio-economic nature in Oaxaca [where] very few people have access to English education, beside the one offered in public schools. For that reason many students begin the program with limited English or just beginning English or emergent English … [The] program requires the students to learn the language but also pedagogical aspects of the program. So [transborder] students … they sort of have a head start.
>
> *—Professor López-Gopar*

This policy of not assessing the English level of applicants is intended to equalize the opportunity for all applicants because it does not favor those whose socio-economic status or migratory experiences give them access to a stronger English education than what Mexican public schools typically offer. Still, the university's broader application process, including the formal entrance exam, which is in Spanish, and the informal influence of government and university officials, favors students with more developed Spanish skills, influential connections, and higher socio-economic status. The process not only removes any English privilege transborder students may have, it can work against them. However, those transborder students who make it into the language education program have an advantage over many of their peers, who must learn or improve their English while simultaneously taking classes on pedagogy and conduct research for a comprehensive thesis that must be written in English. Only students with a 9.5 GPA out of 10 are waived from the thesis requirement.

The language program places students in groups according to English ability so instruction can be geared toward their needs. However, even this categorization does not sufficiently challenge transborder students. I observed Erik in an advanced English language class with five other students. The instructor asked students to speak from the front of the room about a familiar subject. One

132 Issues Impacting Students

student spoke about cats, another talked about what she called the "Tour Eiffel" (Erik encouraged her to say "Eiffel Tower" for the remainder of her speech). He listened attentively to each student, asked questions, and even helped them answer questions from peers when they were stuck. He spoke last. He talked about his favorite soccer player, Cristiano Ronaldo. Unlike the other students, who appeared to speak spontaneously, Erik had done some research and read from notes. His presentation style was relaxed and conversational. He sat on the teacher's desk swinging his legs, while his classmates had stood, visibly nervous. Erik also spoke longer than his peers, who seemed anxious to get out of the spotlight and to stop speaking English. After class, I asked Erik for his thoughts on the session. While I assumed the class was not pedagogically beneficial for him, he said he liked it a lot. He explained that in other classes they've been working on grammar, this was a good way for them to practice speaking and to apply what they learned. Like other transborder students, he felt he needed to learn grammar because he hadn't done so before, and he thought it would help him become a better teacher.

Erik's proficiency and comfort with English was significantly more pronounced than that of his Mexican-educated peers. However, he never appeared boastful about his English; to the contrary, he supported his classmates whenever possible. Another of Erik's professors talked about a moment where Erik wanted to take the focus off of himself and direct it to a fellow student who had learned her English in Mexico:

> There was one gracious thing … another student studied at a private language school, and I was using Erik [to give an example] and he deferred to his classmate who I didn't know she was OK in English. He mentioned her by name and of course she did it so that was interesting. Here's the person who learned all his English in the US and another student who learned all her English in Oaxaca. There was a gracious gesture and the fact he would do that. Maybe he's trying to say there are no borders, I learned in the US but someone can learn it here too if they work at it. They can learn it just as well as I learned it.

Although transborder students may stand out because of their experiences with English in the US, it does not mean they will leave their peers behind. Erik's behavior shows how they can not only serve as models and supports to their classmates, but also advocate for them to be in positions where they are also the models. And it's also a reminder that English should not be a language that is associated with any given country, a salient point for language teachers in Mexico.

Transnational Higher Education Plans

Each developmental group in this study had different realities and plans with regard to higher education. The tertiary students were already studying to earn bachelor's degrees to become English language teachers, with some doing so in Mexico because enrolling in the US wasn't an option for them. The secondary students made plans related to studying or working in Mexico after high school. The elementary students—all of whom have dual nationality—have the possibility of continuing their education in Mexico or in the US.

Cost is the prevailing factor when parents consider their children's education. Emanuel, Melany's father, said, "I won't have the money to send my kids to the better colleges or schools … This restaurant, right here probably will help me to get it. But for them that's my worry." While higher education is generally less expensive in Mexico, there are costs, and depending on the socio-economic level of a family, they may be prohibitive. Public universities are affordable, but they are highly competitive, while private colleges are less stringent about admissions but much more expensive. Alberta, the mother of three US-born dual citizens, talked about how the cost of education would affect her children's education:

> Yo ya les juré que algún día se van a ir a su país y les digo a mis hijos que ahí está el army, "Ustedes pueden ir y ahí les van a dar estudios como militares y ojalá que no pase nada y les puede ayudar el gobierno en eso." Porque yo darles una carrera ahí, a uno a lo mejor pero a todos es mucho dinero.
>
> [I swore to them that they will go back to their country one day. I tell them they can join the army and hopefully nothing happens to them. Then they can study with help from the government. I can't afford to pay for all of their studies, maybe just for one of them, but not all three.]

Alberta refers to the US as "su país" or "their country" when she speaks of her children and is aware of the ways that US citizens have access to free higher education through scholarships or via the armed forces. Her daughters, however, had different plans. They said that after high school they both wanted to be artists in Mexico and teach children how to paint and draw. But at the time of the interview, a decade stood between their childhood plans and the reality of their potential entry into higher education and future place of residency.

Comparison Across Levels

From preschool through high school, many students spend the majority of their waking hours in school with their educators and classmates. As much as educational institutions instill formal knowledge, they also shape how students view the world and create value systems, both explicitly and implicitly. When transborder students move between schools across and even within countries, their understanding of educational systems and nations expands (Hamann et al., 2017). However, this movement is often made even more complicated by educators. Galván said her transbordered life was "perceived [by teachers] as a hindrance to my schooling experience and reflective of my parents' lack of commitment to

FIGURE 6.7 Axianeydt, who loves to draw, sits in her bedroom and shows off her sketchbook of horses (2015).

their daughter's education" (Galván, 2011, p. 553). Yet while educators tend to problematize transborder students and assign blame to their family members for the global forces and economic realities that shaped their lives, they simultaneously place value on the experiences of more privileged students who have the resources to cross borders and partake in study-abroad programs. However, the experiences of these two subgroups are closely aligned in that they both lead to expanded world views, language learning, and opportunities for cross-cultural understanding.

Among the different levels of transborder students, elementary students have less difficulties adjusting to Mexico as compared to their older counterparts and the most opportunity for studying across countries in the future. The elementary students in this study had 0–2 years of schooling in the US, their birthplace, so when they started elementary school in Mexico, they adapted more easily either because it was their first formal school experience or because being a student was still relatively new to them. Those who attended schools in English in the US had not studied Spanish even though they spoke it at home, so in Mexico they were learning to read and write in Spanish alongside their Mexican-born peers. US-born transborder elementary students may blend in at school, but there is one significant difference that separates them from Mexican-born transborder students: their dual nationality. If they have the familial and the financial support, they can continue their studies in the US at the secondary or tertiary level. Attending college in the US, however, requires a level of English that Mexican public schools rarely offer (Despagne & Jacobo, 2016). Still, setting aside financial or language challenges, their learning and living opportunities are much more expansive than those of their older peers.

Among all the transborder students in this study, the secondary students struggled the most in their transition to Mexican schools. They all began their formal education in the US, as part of English monolingual programs, in spite of being multilingual themselves. They returned to Mexico in middle school and found the adjustment to the customs, reading, and writing in Spanish across the content areas, and the lack of support structures, to be a significant challenge. Like the elementary students, they were able to blend in with peers, but they stood out to their teachers as struggling students. Mexican educators were unaware of this unique population because this subgroup was not part of their teacher education or professional development. As a result, students or their families had to advocate for understanding and support related to literacy in Spanish and new learning content, such as history taught from the Mexican perspective. Secondary students experienced a continuum from bullying to admiration related to living in the US and speaking English. Nevertheless, their US experiences were central to their post-high school plans in Mexico, just as they strongly factored into the education experiences of the tertiary students.

Some transborder students returned to Mexico specifically to pursue higher education. Just as gaining entry into a university in the US as an undocumented student is challenging, the same is true when students return to Mexico, even though they are citizens. Most transborder youth are not able to attend post-secondary institutions; those who are admitted to public universities in Mexico are in the minority. For those who major in English language education, like the students in this study, their professors and Mexican-educated classmates quickly took note of their established English practices. Yet they struggle to learn the metalinguistic aspects about the English language well enough to be able to explain them as teachers. Transborder youth have been recognized as a resource to Mexico's teaching of English force, as evidenced by the emergence of teacher preparation programs geared toward their backgrounds. While the country and its future may be fortunate to have this opportunity, English education is not

136 Issues Impacting Students

necessarily a true passion of transborder college students. For some it's the only field for which they feel adequately prepared to study, given other areas require a strong Spanish literacy they did not acquire in US schools.

Education is a right that transcends both national borders and legal boundaries. Yet, school systems and universities in the US and Mexico still have much to do in order to fully acknowledge the needs of transborder students, provide the resources to meet these needs, and build upon the life experiences and language practices transborder students bring to their learning. The next section addresses the larger policy and pedagogy reforms that are necessary to ensure that these students receive an equitable education regardless of country or status.

Note

1 South Carolina eventually allowed DACA recipients to attend public colleges, but Yauzin left the state prior to the start of the program.

References

Alfaro, C., & Gándara, P. (2021). Binational teacher preparation: Constructing pedagogical bridges for the students we share. In P. Gándara and B. Jensen (Eds.), *The students we share: Preparing US and Mexican teachers for our transnational future* (pp. 45–69). SUNY Press.

Bybee, E. R., Jensen, B., & Johnstun, K. (2021). Normalista perspectives on preparing Mexican teachers for American Mexican students. In P. Gándara and B. Jensen (Eds.), *The students we share: Preparing US and Mexican teachers for our transnational future* (pp. 71–96). SUNY Press.

Camera, L. (2016, January 5). The increase in immigrant students test tolerance. *US-News.* www.usnews.com/news/blogs/data-mine/articles/2016-01-05/number-of-immigrant-tudents-is-growing.

Carreón, G. P., Drake, C., & Barton, A. C. (2005). The importance of presence: Immigrant parents' school engagement experiences. *American Educational Research Journal, 42* (3), 465–498.

CEMABE (2014). Secretaría de Educación Pública. Censo de Escuelas, Maestros y Alumnos en Educación Básica. http://cemabe.inegi.org.mx/Reporte.aspx.

Cioè-Peña, M. (2020). Raciolinguistics and the education of emergent bilinguals labeled as disabled. *Urban Review.* doi:10.1007/s11256-11020-00581-z.

Cortez Román, N. A., & Hamann, E. T. (2014). College dreams à la Mexicana… agency and strategy among American-Mexican transnational students. *Latino Studies, 12*(2), 237–258.

Délano Alonso, A. (2018). *From here and there: Diaspora policies, integration and social rights beyond borders.* Oxford University Press.

Despagne, C. & Jacobo, M. (2016). Desafíos actuales de la escuela monolítica mexicana: el caso de los alumnos migrantes transnacionales. *Sinética*, 47.

Ezpeleta, J., & Weiss, E. (1996). Las escuelas rurales en zonas de pobreza y sus maestros: tramas preexistentes y políticas innovadoras. *Revista Mexicana de Investigación Educativa*, 1 (1), 53–69.

Galván, R.T. (2011). Chicana transborder vivencias and autoherteorías: Reflections from the field. *Qualitative Inquiry*, 17(6), 552–557.

Gándara, P., & Contreras, F. (2009). *The Latino education crisis: The consequences of failed social policies.* Harvard University Press.

Gomez, M.N., & Diarrassouba, N. (2014). What do teachers need to support English learners? *English Language Teaching,* 7(5), 89–101.

Hamel, R. E. (2008). Indigenous language policy and education in Mexico. In S. May & N. H. Hornberger (Eds.), *Encyclopedia of language and education,* 2nd ed. (1: pp. 301–313). Springer.

Hamann, E. T., Perez, W., Gallo, S., & Zúñiga, V. (2017). The students we share: US teachers' responsibilities given that some of their students will later go to school in Mexico. http://glec.education.iupui.edu/Images/Briefs/hamann_immigrantstudents.pdf.

Hurn, C. J. (1993). *The limits and possibilities of schooling: An introduction to the sociology of education.* Pearson College Division.

INEE (2018). *Panorama educativo de México 2017.* Instituto Nacional para la Evaluación de la Educación.

Jensen, B. (2021). Equitable teaching enhances achievement opportunity for the students we share. In P. Gándara & B. Jensen (Eds.), *The students we share: Preparing US and Mexican teachers for our transnational future* (pp. 145–174). SUNY Press.

Kleyn, T. & García, O. (2019). Translanguaging as an act of transformation: Restructuring teaching and learning for emergent bilinguals. In L. de Oliveira (Ed.), *The Handbook of TESOL in K-12* (pp. 69–82). Wiley-Blackwell.

Kleyn, T. & Stern N. (2018). Labels as limitations. *MinneTESOL Journal.* http://minnete soljournal.org/spring-2018/labels-as-limitations.

López-Gopar, M. E. (2014). Teaching English critically to Mexican children. *ELT Journal,* 68(3), 310–320.

López-Gopar, M. E. (2016). *Decolonizing primary English language teaching.* Multilingual Matters.

Mangual Figueroa, A. (2013). Citizenship and language education policy in an emerging Latino community in the United States. *Language Policy,* 12, 333–354.

Martínez, I. (2019). *Becoming transnational youth workers: Independent Mexican teenage migrants and pathways of survival and social mobility.* Rutgers University Press.

Medina, D., & Menjívar, C. (2015). The context of return migration: challenges of mixed-status families in Mexico's schools. *Ethnic and Racial Studies,* 38(12), 2123–2139.

Otros Dreams en Acción (2017, October 7). Teaching English may not have been "your dream" before deportation/return, heck, it may not be your dream [Status update]. www.facebook.com/OtrosDreams/posts/1391539504307011.

Ramirez, A. F. (2003). Dismay and disappointment: Parental involvement of Latino immigrant parents. *The Urban Review,* 35(2), 93–110.

Román González, B., & Sánchez García, J. (2021). Mirroring students' and teachers' classroom experiences to address the challenges of transnationalism in Mexican schools. In P. Gándara & B. Jensen (Eds.), *The students we share: Preparing US and Mexican teachers for our transnational future* (pp. 175–197). SUNY Press.

Santibañez, L. (2021). Contrasting realities: How differences between the Mexican and US education systems affect transnational students. In P. Gándara & B. Jensen (Eds.), *The students we share: Preparing US and Mexican teachers for our transnational future* (pp. 17–44). SUNY Press.

Sayer, P., & López-Gopar, M. E. (2016). Language education in Mexico. In W. E. Wright, S. Boun, & O. García (Eds.), *The handbook of bilingual and multilingual education* (pp. 578–591). John Wiley & Sons. doi:10.1002/9781118533406.ch37.

Schissel, J. L., & Reyes, M. (2020). Preparing to teach emergent bilinguals: Examining practices and shifting language ideologies of non-ESL preservice educators. *Journal of Multilingual Theories and Practices*, 1(2), 290–312.

Secretaría de Educación Pública (2008). *Mientras llego a mi escuela/While I arrive to school*. Secretaría de Educación Pública.

Tian, Z., Aghai, L., Sayer, P., & Schissel, J. L. (Eds.) (2020). *Envisioning TESOL through a translanguaging lens: Global perspectives*. Springer Nature.

Turner, E.O. & Mangual Figueroa, A. (2019). Immigration policy and education in lived reality: A framework for researchers and educators. *Educational Researcher*. doi:10.3102/0013189X19872496.

US Department of Education (2015). *Resource guide: Supporting undocumented youth*. US Department of Education.

Van Dam, A. (2019). Teacher strikes made 2018 the biggest year for worker protest in a generation. *The Washington Post*. www.washingtonpost.com/us-policy/2019/02/14/with-teachers-lead-more-workers-went-strike-than-any-year-since/.

Zúñiga, V., Hamann, E. T., & Sánchez García, J. (2008). *Alumnos transnacionales: las escuelas mexicanas frente a la globalización*. Secretaría de Educación Pública.

PART III

Lessons Learned

7
POLICY AND PEDAGOGY IMPLICATIONS

FIGURE 7.1 When Sharely, left, and her sister, Nancy, moved with their mother and father to Oaxaca from California, they first lived in a small home made of tin on the edge of their parents' rural hometown, San Juan Guelavía (2015).

The right to emigrate—to leave one's native country—is enshrined as a basic principle in the United Nations Universal Declaration of Human Rights. In the southern Mexican state of Oaxaca, where three out of every four people live in extreme poverty, where conditions have worsened since the enactment of NAFTA, and

DOI: 10.4324/9780429340178-10

142 Lessons Learned

where a substantial portion of the population left for the United States, people have taken to demanding another right: the right *not* to migrate—that is, to stay home and enjoy a modicum of comfort and dignity, free from exploitation.

—Henderson, 2011, p. 157

There is an urgent need to create humane policies and equitable pedagogical practices for the 9 million Mexican-origin "students we share" in Pre-K-12 schools between the US and Mexico. Of those, 2 million have lived in both Mexico and the US and 800,000 are US-citizen or US-educated students in the Mexican educación básica system (Gándara & Jensen, 2021; Hamann et al., 2020). Each of those students is part of a larger family; thus, the shared population between the two countries is even larger. These families are often divided by artificial and shifting borders that denote countries, which grant some people the privilege to cross them and deny that opportunity to others. Nevertheless, people make and remake their lives in places where governmental policies determine the extent to which one can live and move freely.

Migration is central to the lives of transborder children and young people. It affects their sense of self and both connects and disconnects them with family and peers. Border crossings dramatically change schooling experiences, alter language practices, and build in-depth understanding of local, national, and transnational migration policies through personal experiences. This phenomenon is common between the US and Mexico as contiguous neighbors, but by no means is exclusive to these countries. It is a global reality that touches nearly every country as political, economic, and environmental forces uproot families, pushing and pulling them across borders with their children.

Migration is linked inextricably to policies that span the binaries of dehumanization and dignity, access and denial, and constructs of "legality" and "illegality." These policies are ultimately personal, dictating how people live their lives and the extent to which they can fulfill their goals. This final chapter connects the stories and experiences of the transborder students, their families, and their educators to policies and pedagogies that will improve the experiences and trajectories of people who live and learn between the US, Mexico, and beyond. It considers transnational and national policies that will enhance the lives and educational experiences of people who migrate. It also provides an overview of pedagogical approaches that school systems and educators from elementary, secondary, and tertiary levels can enact to advance the schooling for transborder students. Ideally, these pedagogies will be implemented hand-in-hand with policy changes, but they will be useful even outside of large-scale reforms.

Policy Recommendations

Political, economic, and social policies—or their absence—often allow those with privilege to sustain and expand their power and resources while dispossessing marginalized groups. These policies subsequently force people to migrate by making their daily lives so difficult that their survival hangs in the balance. The impact of these policies is felt from the local level, where an international trade agreement may damage the ability of a farmer to make a living, to the state to the national to the binational and the transnational, where immigration laws grant passage to citizens of one country and not to another. The recommendations provided here range from the aspirational, seemingly impossible to realize in the world as it stands, to the practical and immediately do-able. A full range of pro- posals is important and necessary in order to be able to take small steps forward with actionable policies while working toward a larger vision for the future. This "both/and" approach allows for short-term changes that are not monumental, but can improve aspects of people's lives while moving toward more challenging goals that work towards liberation and counter the enduring legacy of colonialism.

Transnational Policies

Transnational policies address the interconnectedness of countries and their poli- tical, economic, and social systems. These policies are particularly important for countries in the same region or continent, where a confluence of forces can have a widespread impact on people who are physically close yet politically separated by borders that were created and recreated for specific purposes. Transnational policies can be especially detrimental to poorer nations or those who are already marginalized (the negative impacts of NAFTA on the Mexican economy is one example). Therefore, prioritizing under-resourced nations and specifically the most oppressed groups within them is where transnational policies would truly cultivate change.

Deregulation of National Borders

Highly controlled and regulated borders between countries have become the global norm over the past three centuries. However, it doesn't have to be this way. The elimination or reduction of regulations across borders would permit the unrestricted movement of people from country to country, instead of the situation that exists now where that privilege is only available to a small portion of the population. People would be able to be with their family members, find employment where they are needed, and be able to travel to their country of origin if they are working elsewhere. While this approach would open numerous opportunities, it would simultaneously end the il/leg- ality of migration and close businesses and government industries that profit off of unjust migration policies.

While the open movement of people is hard to imagine, it does happen presently, albeit in more limited ways. The European Union (EU) allows for the movement of

144 Lessons Learned

citizens under the Schengen Area, consisting primarily but not exclusively of members of the EU, maintains open borders for 400 million people to travel, work, and live among its member nations. In North America, the US-Canada border is permeable, allowing two-way flow for passport holders between the countries with few restrictions to travel between the two nations. By contrast, the Mexico-US border is militarized and strongly favors US passport holders. The US requires Mexican citizens to navigate extra and costly steps that still often lead to the denial of their movement north. Espindola and Jacobo-Suárez (2018, p. 56) discuss the "right of return or, even a right to circulate" for Mexicans, especially given that US territory was taken from Mexico. Circulation has been at the heart of migration patterns for people whose work and family lives have been between the two countries. Further, the right to circulate does not require people to select one country over the other, but live more fully and freely between both.

Cooperative Policies Focusing on the Most Vulnerable Countries and Groups

Transnational economic policies either facilitate or inhibit the capacity of people to meet their basic needs and support their families. Transnational policies with an eye toward the bottom line (i.e., dollars or pesos), without a focus on social and human impacts and equitable outcomes for marginalized groups, only serve to reproduce inequities and force migration, both internally, from rural to urban areas, and externally. Refocusing these policies requires addressing the needs of the most vulnerable populations, rather than prioritizing corporate profits that take advantage of the labor and resources with little to no benefit for them. But if transnational policies put cooperation over competition and look beyond artificial borders with a view toward humanity as interconnected and international, then migration can become a choice, and part of which would be "the right to not migrate" (Bacon, 2014).[1]

These recommendations require a seismic shift in the development of transnational policies and their goals. But it is only through the collaboration of nations—especially when focusing on the flows of people across borders—that large scale inequities within and between countries can ultimately diminish.

National Policies

National policies greatly affect quality of life and opportunity—or lack thereof. If these policies create conditions that are essentially unlivable, that is depriving someone of their ability to sustain themself of their family, they can force people to migrate. When economic, social, and educational policies (the next section addresses the latter) support the most marginalized, they have the power to reverse inequities when they are backed up by action and funding. The policy recommendations outlined here for Mexico and the US build from the experiences of the transborder families in this study.

Mexican Policies

Poverty Reduction Measures

A consistent reason Mexicans head north to the US is poverty, driven by the lack of means to meet their basic needs (Elsasser, 2018). Economic policies can intervene in this reality by creating the conditions to allow people to live a stable life that does not force them to migrate. Although transnational policies can have a larger influence on economies, national policies can also be important and meaningful, such as those that support local workforce development, the creation of jobs that pay a livable rate, and increases in the minimum wage for those working in the formal sector. Further, the development of safety nets that provide food, healthcare and shelter for people who are unemployed or underemployed, disabled, or elderly would also allow Mexicans to feel secure and supported in difficult times.

Reacclimation Support

To ease the reacclimation of families who return to Mexico, the country needs more robust national policies and support systems. While governmental organizations such as the Instituto Oaxaqueño de Atención al Migrante (IOAM) operate across Mexican states, their impact is limited due to insufficient funding; they do not have the money to assist the growing numbers of transborder families in the country. Délano Alonso has noted Mexican migrants receive more support from Mexican consulates in the US than they do from the government when they return to their country of origin. "Mexico is helping migrants become members of a country where they are not citizens," she found, "while denying their membership in the country where they do hold citizenship" (2018, p. 168). Funding governmental agencies *in* Mexico *for* Mexicans is essential. Agencies need the staff to provide support that includes assistance in receiving national documentation to apply for employment, information about job opportunities where they can apply the skills and experiences they acquired in the US, and help with getting a driver's license, healthcare, and schooling. Additionally, the families of US-born children may need assistance with the process of doble nacionalidad in order to more easily access resources in Mexico. Finally, up-to-date information about all of these tools and services needs to be readily available online, as well as distributed via pamphlets, television, radio, and social media.

146 Lessons Learned

Non-governmental Organization Funding

The government has a large role to play in the repatriation of transborder families, but it cannot do this work alone. Non-governmental organizations—especially those headed by people directly impacted by return migration, who have the deepest understanding of this community's realities and needs—are critical in this work. One example of such an organization is Otros Dreams en Acción (ODA), co-founded by Maggie Loredo and Jill Anderson. ODA is "dedicated to mutual support and political action for and by those who grew up in the United States and now find themselves in Mexico due to deportation, the deportation of a family member, or the threat of deportation" (n.d.). Although the organization is active online, its physical location is the Poch@ House, "a cultural space based in Mexico City that celebrates and reclaims a new hybrid and multifaceted culture in Mexico, one of Spanglish, of exile, and of claiming belonging aquí y allá" (ODA, n.d.). ODA is an example of the type of organizations needed across Mexico for families and young people to feel connected and supported over the long-term and in ways that go beyond official governmental processes.

US Policies

Transborder families in the US experience a nation that differs from popular conceptions by media-driven images where money grows on trees and everyone lives in luxury. For undocumented immigrants in particular, the reality they face cannot be further from this fantasy. The US has a combination of federal and state policies and programs that frequently make life more challenging for those without papers as well as limit their opportunities and restrict the liminal spaces in which they can feel slightly safer. To fully acknowledge the humanity of all people living on the land, a significant shift in federal policy is needed, one that is more wide-reaching. Current attempts at beneficial immigration policy changes tend to focus on smaller subgroups—such as those referred to as "DREAMers"—while their family members continue to suffer at the hands of the government.

Abolish ICE and Immigrant Detention

The criminalization of immigrants and militarization of immigrant policy in the US is most visible at the southern border and through the nationwide activities of Immigration and Customs Enforcement (ICE). Abolishing ICE, which was formed in 2003, would free undocumented immigrants from the constant state of surveillance and fear in which they now live. The billions of dollars spent annually on ICE could be redirected to supporting immigrants in the US and into distributing international aid that could improve the conditions of people in Mexico and elsewhere where US interference has caused significant hardship, reducing the economic imperative to migrate. Furthermore, the US can close immigrant detention centers, which wrongly criminalize people who are escaping global forces, conflicts and natural disasters that endanger their lives and livelihoods.

Large-Scale Regularization and Circulation

In the absence of large-scale immigration reform over the last few decades, the US has become a patchwork of federal programs with a limited reach and an erratic array of state-level policies that are a mix of pro- and anti-immigrant measures. To rectify this dysfunctional and untenable array of policies and programs, a range of federal actions are needed. First, all immigrants living in the country without authorization must be permitted to regularize their status so they can attain full membership in society as both contributors and beneficiaries. This action should be done outside of criteria for age, country of origin, or the extent to which one can benefit the US. As humans they deserve to belong, especially on land that has a history of being stolen twice, initially from Indigenous Peoples by the Spanish who colonized Mexico, and then again when the US took it from Mexico. Next, there is a need for a more equitable immigration policy, one that is not based on economic means and connections and instead permits for people of all origins to enter (and circulate within) the US. A small-scale yet significant policy around the right to circulate would be to allow US citizen children living abroad to return to the US without a passport, especially if their families cannot afford the application or renewal fees.

Increased Rights for Undocumented Immigrants

Until undocumented immigrants are able to live with dignity as fully recognized residents or citizens of the country, other measures could enable them to live more freely. Currently, states control access undocumented immigrants have to health insurance, drivers licenses, higher education, and financial aid. This piecemeal approach makes people's lives unnecessarily difficult. *Plyler v. Doe*, the 1982 case that requires all students in the US the right to a public K–12 education, regardless of status, provides a useful precedent for policy approaches. The haphazard set of state-by-state laws and regulations that complicate the lives of immigrants could be made more orderly, and therefore more beneficial, by federal actions that provide access to the rights and entitlements now denied to many people, especially those living in states with stringent anti-immigrant policies.

Pedagogy Policy and Practice Recommendations

FIGURE 7.2 Yauzin, teaching English to a class of primary school students in Oaxaca (2015).

> When any two (or more) countries are immersed in migratory flows ... they have a *shared duty* of justice toward the children of returned migrants.
>
> —Espindola & Jacobo-Suárez, 2018, p. 55

Although education is referred to as a human right, not all children and youth have access to it. When migration intersects with education the results can range from a truncation of schooling to an expansion of educational opportunities. In rural Mexico, some students must choose migration over education as a way to support their families from afar (Meyers, 2014). In the US, undocumented students can complete high school, but some states prevent them from attending public colleges or require them to pay out-of-state tuition and exclude them from financial aid. Transborder families with US-educated students encounter bureaucratic barricades in Mexico that hinder access to schools and colleges. While there are differences across nations, the one constant is the mismatch between the relatively static nature of schools and the mobility of students (Zúñiga & Hamann, 2008). This results in an education that may be locally relevant, but inconsistent with the complex trajectories of students' lives. Furthermore, "the knowledge, understandings and perspectives that these children need...cannot be understood in mononational terms" (Hamann & Zúñiga, 2021, p. 101).

Transnational Policies and Pedagogies

Multilateral Agreements

Movement across and within countries often fragments the education of transborder students. Each relocation activates systems that have tedious admissions requirements, new languages of instruction, curriculum that values different types of knowledge and perspectives, and varied behavioral norms and traditions. Given the flows of families across borders, it makes sense for nations who share students to come together to make the education of transborder students as seamless as possible. A transnational agreement between Mexico and the US would significantly improve the quality and consistency of the education of transborder students. It would start with a binational dialogue that puts forth "a clear statement of our shared responsibility to provide an equitable education for these students" (Gándara & Jensen, 2021, p. 256). Then attention could be focused on areas such as a seamless transfer of documents, teacher exchanges, sharing of textbooks and resources, and guidance about transborder students for educators and families, as just a few examples. Such a collaboration is certainly not an easy undertaking, especially because the US delegates school control to the states, while Mexico employs a centralized system. Nevertheless, school systems and nations cannot ignore cyclical migrations that affect the quality of education transborder students receive.

Teacher Preparation and Education Shifts

Although schools cannot single-handedly override oppressive policies and deep-rooted poverty—nor should they be solely responsible to do so—educators hold tremendous power to positively (or negatively) affect a student's learning and sense of self. Hanushek (2016) found that teacher quality is key to student achievement. Therefore, it is critical that teachers begin their careers with a deep understanding of migration issues and the approaches to support transborder students academically, linguistically, and socio-emotionally. To develop this capacity, teacher education programs must emphasize the connection between education, language, and migration at the local, national, and transnational level. No matter the grade level or content area, programs must address the interrelations and histories of countries students circulate between. Academic texts, films, and stories are useful in addressing these topics, but binational collaborations— even virtual ones—that bring together students and educators go a step further by enabling the real-time sharing of experiences and approaches. Teachers, both pre- and in-service, would gain valuable insight into their transborder students by participating in international practicum-based experiences in the schools of the countries their students are coming from or returning to. Even more powerful are binational programs that prepare teachers from Mexico and the US (for examples

150 Lessons Learned

see Chapter 6). Teachers with these experiences would be better positioned to integrate pedagogies, histories, and languages between the neighboring nations into their instructional practices.

Building Up Bilingual Programs

Refining—or even revolutionizing—teacher education to be responsive to the realities of transborder students is important, but it is not enough. The creation of programs that allow for learning that is inclusive of students' full linguistic repertoire in public Pre-K through high school must start from a translanguaging stance to ensure that transborder students are allowed and encouraged to access—rather than repress—their full linguistic repertoire (García et al., 2017; Menken & Sánchez, 2019). This will allow them to experience linguistic freedom and justice in their education as they are better able to access content and make sense of their migration journeys (España & Herrera, 2020). The greater availability of bilingual programs would allow students to more seamlessly live, study, and eventually work across countries. At a minimum, transborder students who move between Mexico and the US should have access to both Spanish and English as the languages of instruction. Indigenous languages should also be a part of their schooling, especially if students have speakers of these languages in their families. The challenge for most countries lies in the recruitment of bilingual teachers (Gándara, 2016). Transborder students themselves are one way to address this teacher shortage as ideal candidates who are bilingual individuals who have also lived across nations and cultures.

Education for Global Citizenship

Transborder students are not tied to any single nation and will continue to live mobile lives. It is insufficient for schools to educate these students solely for membership of the country in which they currently reside. Their futures require them to have multinational links, both physically and, increasingly, virtually. Preparing students to live in the larger world is not easy, but it is important to respond to the flows of people and ideas that will surely continue and likely intensify throughout the 21st century. Bokova proposes educating students by thinking beyond borders and national citizenship:

> Global citizenship is not a legal term, but rather one that indicates a sense of solidarity with others to share the wealth of diversity as a force of renewal, not one of distrust. Educating global citizens is about empowering young men and women to live in a world under pressure, with human rights and dignity as the starting point for all action. This education must be taught from the earliest age to nurture cultural and linguistic diversity as forces of belonging and innovation.
>
> *—Bokova, 2019, p. 213*

Critical Dialogic Education

Teaching toward global citizenship requires educational policies that build connections between countries, prioritize programs that are reflective of students' linguistic repertoires, and approach teaching about current immigration issues in a manner that allows students to look at history, policies, and lived experiences through a multifaceted and critical lens. Categorizing migration and return migration as "good" or "bad" is neither helpful nor productive. Instead, the focus of instruction should be to invite students to explore this complicated and ever-changing phenomenon with the intent of understanding how it is influenced by global forces and transnational policies that empower some and disenfranchise others. Instead, critical dialogic education can center students' voices and experiences as a way to develop nuanced understandings of complex issues, such as migration (Kibler et al., 2021). A study by Dina López and I in New York City high schools where teachers enacted this approach with immigrant and US-born students found:

> The key dialogic features of this pedagogy … included meaningful collaboration across the content areas to develop robust interdisciplinary units, the use of multimodal sources with heteroglossic perspectives, and an emphasis on transcending the students' singular experiences with current immigration issues.
> —*Kleyn & López, 2021, p. 312*

This approach is important for *all* students, even those without migration in their history, so they are able to better understand those who do migrate and be able to make informed decisions about migration if it enters their own trajectory. Furthermore, critical dialogic education allows multilingual and multicultural transborder students to make important contributions through their experiential understanding of the ways in which unjust policies impact families who migrate. They are in a unique position to educate their peers and teachers about their lived realities across countries, languages, cultures, and school systems if they feel safe and comfortable in doing so.

Teaching Migration through Multimodal Resources

Multimodal resources are useful to start critical conversations about migration with students. The short documentary in which some of the transborder students and families in this study participated, *Una Vida, Dos Países: Children and Youth (Back) in Mexico* (Kleyn et al., 2016) and its accompanying Spanish-English bilingual curriculum, includes lessons that address identity, languaging, economics, and policies between the US and Mexico for secondary students (Kleyn, n.d.). Children's literature also provides a powerful place from which to launch critical conversations with young students about difficult topics. Books such as *Areli is a Dreamer: A True Story*

152 Lessons Learned

(Morales & Uribe, 2021), *Mama the Alien/Mamá la extraterrestre* (Lainez, 2017), and *El Muro/The Wall* (Kemmeter, 2005) allow students to situate migration beyond individual circumstances to see how governmental forces affect the movements and treatment of people across borders.

Immigrant Justice School Clubs

Outside of formal classroom structures, there are ways for transborder students to connect to one another and advocate for their communities. Student clubs are opportunities for directly impacted students, peer allies and accomplices to come together. In Mexico, the "New Dreamers," featured in the *Una Vida, Dos Países* film (see unavidathefilm.com) is an example of how transborder students make themselves more visible as they share experience and even practice English in a way that is more natural than in a class for new English speakers. In the US, "Dream Teams" or immigrant justice groups have formed in middle schools, high schools, and colleges that enable students to connect, share resources, and push for immigration reform in their schools, states, country and beyond. One organization that has built structures and supports for young people working to start such clubs is the New York State Youth Leadership Council (see www.nysylc.org). The CUNY-Initiative on Immigration and Education (CUNY-IIE) has developed a professional development module that supports educators in considering if Dream Teams are a fit for their school (Diaz-Granados et al., 2021). Established school groups can amplify their impact by connecting and collaborating with each other across secondary and tertiary levels, both nationally and transnationally to fully reflect the lives of transborder students.

National Policies and Pedagogies

Mexican Policies and Pedagogies

The Mexican education system does little to account for transborder students in policy or practice. Instead of honoring these students for the rich experiences and understandings they bring to schools, administrators and teachers often view them through a mononational lens that positions them as struggling learners. Hamann & Zúñiga (2011) found that rather than receiving the support they need as they acclimate to learning through a new language and culture, transborder students were three times more likely to be retained in a grade compared to their Mexican born and educated peers. The remedy for this situation calls for a combination of teacher education, school-based policies, and practices that highlight the strengths of transborder students and provides them support to succeed.

Building Awareness of Transborder Students

An initial step is creating an awareness that transborder students are part of the Mexican school system and that they have strengths and challenges that may differ from those of their peers. Teacher education programs ranging from the escuelas normales (or teachers' colleges) to the Universidad Pedagógica Nacional (UPN) as well as public and private universities must ensure that this growing subgroup is a part of the curriculum for all educators across levels and subject areas. A promising sign of movement in this direction is the book, *Lo que los maestros de México necesitan conocer sobre la educación básica en las escuelas de Estados Unidos* (Hamann et al., forthcoming). This edited volume published by UPN includes chapters written by US educators and translated into Spanish by Mexican scholars that describe the education experiences of Mexican-origin students in US schools. They range from explaining how English literacy instruction is approached to the experiences of a mixed-status family in New York City whose children attend either a bilingual education program, English as a new language classes, or a specialized high school for immigrant youth. Understanding the experiences students bring from the US is key to not only raise the visibility of this group, but also to enable teachers to meet students where they are in order to create supportive learning environments in which they can grow academically, linguistically, and socio-emotionally.

Professional Development for Teachers

While it's important to ensure that new teachers have an awareness and understanding of how to support transborder students, there are many practicing educators who have not had the opportunity to learn about these students even though they are already in their classrooms. The *Guía de apoyo a docentes con estudiantes transfronterizos: alumnos de educación básica y media superior* (Kleyn & The New Dreamer del CETis 124, 2015) is one tool that breaks down approaches to educate transborder students in the following areas: (1) stories of transborder students, (2) socio-emotional supports, (3) pedagogy in Spanish, and (4) English growth. The guide was a collaboration with the New Dreamers—which included Sharely, Melchor, and Brayan—at their Oaxacan high school, CETis 124, and graduate students in language education at the Universidad Autónoma Benito Juárez de Oaxaca (UABJO). It is a tool that can guide conversations within schools as teachers can try out the suggested strategies with transborder students. Ideally, there could be professional development sessions about these students or teacher-led study groups that build awareness, leading to changes in practices and policies that acknowledge the existence, resources, and needs of transborder students in Mexican schools.

Spanish Support Classes

Learning in and through Spanish is an obstacle many transborder students and their teachers name as a key challenge. If bilingual education (as mentioned in

154 Lessons Learned

the transnational policy section) is not feasible, transborder students may require access to instruction that is connected to learning literacy and content in Spanish. Such programs would be similar to those for students learning English in the US, but should not be monolingual spaces that police students' languaging, but rather, provide opportunities for them to express themselves freely and learn through a translanguaging pedagogy (García et al, 2017).

Inclusion of Indigenous Language and Knowledge

For Indigenous students, having the opportunity to learn through or even about an Indigenous language in addition to Spanish and English is important for their identity and connection to their community, allowing them to bring their full selves into schools. Schools can also support students to draw on their Indigenous knowledge systems by "embedding skills instruction within meaningful and purposeful community contexts and collaborative, communal activities that involve students and familias in authentic, rather than aesthetic, ways" (Urrieta, 2013, p. 332).

Creative Approaches to English Growth

Continued English development is also a challenge for transborder students because they find themselves in rudimentary classes that were developed with beginning learners in mind. One way to meet these needs is through the creation of service learning projects that include community-based language exchanges. Such ventures can be done in partnership with local universities or with community members who themselves have lived between the US and Mexico (Tacelosky, 2013).

These approaches are not easy to enact, but their difficulty makes them no less critical in the education of transborder students. These students require—and deserve—educators who are multilingual and multiliterate or, at minimum, those who are able to trust students to language in ways that are central to their identity and learning. Time will be needed to develop programs that address these gaps in elementary and secondary schools and teacher education institutions. Of course, schools will need more funding to implement these changes, which are essential in order to give transborder students a locally and globally relevant education.

United States Policies and Pedagogies

US schools often subject Mexican students to subtractive schooling that excludes their home culture and language and views those aspects of their identities as problems (Valenzuela, 1999). Further, immigrant students, despite their legal right to an education, have been pushed out of schools to the extent that some

Policy and Pedagogy Implications **155**

newly arrived students are denied entry altogether. School officials persuade them to enroll in high school equivalency programs rather than the traditional high schools so as not to bring down the standardized test scores of a school by which administrators are judged (Lukes, 2015). Some young people become so discouraged with the educational system that they go directly into the workforce. As a result, Mexican-origin students have low high school graduation rates and are the least likely of all racial and ethnic groups to graduate from college (Gándara & Jensen, 2021). Clearly, these outcomes demand significant changes in US policies and pedagogies in order to better serve transborder students and prepare them for their future, whether it be in Mexico, the US, or elsewhere.

Integrating Immigration Issues into Teacher Certification

Ideally, future educators in the US would begin learning about immigration issues and approaches to working with immigrant students and families in teacher education programs. However, there is little discussion about these topics, especially as they relate to documentation and the construction of "illegality" (Jeffries & Dabach, 2014). Most programs outside of bilingual education and TESOL do not offer coursework specifically focused on the migration, linguistic, and academic approaches to teaching immigrant-origin students. Those programs that do focus on multilingual learners, who are immigrants or children of immigrants, address the dynamic cultures of students, their languaging practices, and ways to nurture their linguistic repertoire. Attention is primarily placed on students bureaucratically labeled as "English Language Learners" and their subgroups, including "Students with Limited or Interrupted Formal Education" (SLIFE). This population is defined as having limited access to formal education or breaks in their schooling in their country of origin as a result of migration, war, civil unrest, or poverty (DeCapua & Marshall, 2010). Students labeled as SLIFE bring to schools their migration histories—as asylees, refugees, or undocumented minors who are often unaccompanied by adults (although they often reunite with family members in the US). These histories are central to who they are. This imbalance is largely due to state standards that mandate teaching language and content in teacher education programs, without explicitly addressing immigration.[2] Changes are needed. State education departments should name immigration as a required content area for all teacher education programs that are tied to teaching to the state standards.

Awareness of Mexican Student Diversity

Learning about larger immigration issues is important, but it is equally important that educators understand the histories and ethnolinguistic backgrounds of current immigrant populations. In communities with Mexican immigrants, there is a need

156 Lessons Learned

to understand the diversity that exists within this heterogeneous population. A common misunderstanding is that everyone from Mexico speaks Spanish, and only Spanish. As a result, when bilingual programs are available, Indigenous students may find themselves learning through Spanish and English even if their families mostly speak Mixteco or Zapoteco, for example. In these bilingual settings they struggle to learn through two new languages. This is not to suggest that Indigenous students should not take part in such programs, but that other spaces be created for students to share their Indigenous identity and language practices, and use them as strengths that can be built upon. Indigenous students can also educate their peers (and teachers) about their home languages and the linguistic diversity of the Mexican community. Velasco explains the consequences of overlooking students' rich backgrounds:

> Unless adaptations in pedagogy are made for indigenous children coming from cultures rich in orature and not literacy, these children will fail in school, even in bilingual education programs. In fact, dual-language two-way bilingual education programs, with their emphasis on the "dual," might silence the other languages of the children and obliterate the fact that there may be children from national contexts where Spanish is official but their home languages are other than Spanish. It is thus the pedagogical adaptations made by bilingual teachers that make the difference for these students.
>
> *—Velasco, 2010, p. 269*

Creating Spaces for Indigenous Languages

Furthermore, if transborder children return to Mexico they will be well served by programs where their Indigenous languages and cultures are central to school experiences. Schools with small numbers of Indigenous students whose families speak the same language can start after-school programs led by a community educator (who need not be certified) that allow students to explore their language, culture, and history. This range of approaches will allow transborder students to maintain a foundation from which to connect and communicate with their community and family in Mexico and to feel a sense of pride about their Indigenous roots.

Culturally Sustaining Pedagogies

Given the diversity among immigrant and US-born transborder children, it is important for all students to develop understandings of language and culture that start from their own backgrounds and expand out to those of their school, community, and society. Galda (1998) explains this approach with the metaphor of windows and mirrors within a school's curriculum. Mirrors allow students to see people with similar backgrounds and experiences, while windows provide opportunities to learn about those who are different from them. For transborder students, this means proving windows to migration where it is not only a linear phenomenon, but a historical and present-day cyclical reality for people between the US, Mexico, and other countries. In US schools, however, students of color more often look through windows rather than at mirrors. Their education centers white people and their histories and experiences. Students from minoritized backgrounds are often "othered," their identities relegated to a special month to be celebrated before education resumes its mainstream curriculum (Nieto, 2009). Culturally sustaining pedagogy is an approach that counters the erasure of communities who have been colonized, enslaved, and oppressed in the US (Paris & Alim, 2017). It is an education that values and sustains the dynamic languages, cultures, histories, and literacies of students of color in schools while maintaining accountability to the community, which spans borders for immigrant-origin students.

Conclusion

People always have and always will migrate. Violence, poverty, injustice, and increasingly climate change force them to uproot their lives and replant themselves in new lands. People migrate out of necessity, regardless of whether governmental laws and policies allow them to do so. For some, migration is an unearned privilege, granted by birthplace or economic status; for many others, the right *to* migrate—or to *not* migrate—is a human right for which they struggle. Migrants who are not deemed worthy of belonging to a nation via governmental citizenship must reckon with remaining on land where they are criminalized, or returning to their country of origin and the very conditions that led them to flee. For some, deportation dictates their trajectory; others are coerced, or refuse to submit to policies that restrict their freedoms and strip them of their dignity. As a result, migration does not necessarily produce an end-point. The process is not linear, but cyclical. It can span many countries, occupy years of fears and hopes and border crossings, and forever alter the adults and children who live it.

The transborder students in this book illuminate how cyclical migration can lead to joy, freedom, and opportunity, just as it can also evoke separation, struggle, and resentment. Students living, learning, and languaging between the US and Mexico are often viewed through a bounded cultural and political lens that does not recognize all the parts of their experiences and identities. They are regularly confronted with artificial borders that limit their deep-rooted connections to different languages, cultures, and countries. Government policies, school systems, and public discourse often fail to see these realities and embrace the gifts of transborder students and families. It is only when humanity prevails over narrow and racialized definitions of deservingness and when transnational cooperation triumphs over competition that transborder students will be free to live aquí, allá y más allá (here, there, and beyond).

Notes

1 Although it is beyond the scope of this study, there is a growing need for transnational policy between Mexico, the US, and Central American nations to address the treatment of Central Americans traveling through Mexico en route to the US, as well as those who make Mexico their new home. To learn more about this see Vega (2019), Meyer and Taft-Morales (2019), and Verza (2020).
2 The CUNY-Initiative on Immigration and Education (CUNY-IIE), where I serve as the Principal Investigator, has developed resources for educators to learn about current immigration issues. These materials include the *Supporting Immigrants in Schools* video series and four accompanying professional development modules on the following topics: (1) Key Immigration Issues, (2) Refugees and Immigrants in Schools, (3) Immigration in Elementary Schools, and (4) Immigration in Secondary Schools (see www.cuny-iie.org).

References

Bacon, D. (2014, October 24). Oaxacans want right to (not) migrate. *The Progressive*. https://progressive.org/dispatches/oaxacans-want-right-not-migrate.

Bokova, I. (2019). Empowering global citizens for a just and peaceful world. In M. Suárez-Orozco (Ed.). (pp. 209–217). *Humanitarianism and mass migration: Confronting the world crisis*. University of California Press.

DeCapua, A., & Marshall, H. W. (2010). Serving ELLs with limited or interrupted education: Intervention that works. *TESOL Journal*, 1(1), 49–70.

Délano Alonso, A. (2018). *From here and there: Diaspora policies, integration and social rights beyond borders*. Oxford University Press.

Diaz-Granados, D., Li Zheng, A., Park, C., Queenan, J., & Zaino, K. (2021). Professional development module: Immigration in secondary schools. www.cuny-iie.org/upcoming-work-2.

Elsasser, A. A. (2018). Migration from Mexico to the US: The impacts of NAFTA on Mexico and the United States and what to do going forward. *International Review of Business and Economics*, 2(1), 115–128.

España, C., & Herrera, L. Y. (2020). *En Comunidad: Lessons for centering the voices and experiences of bilingual Latinx students*. Heinemann.

Espindola, J., & Jacobo-Suárez, M. (2018). The ethics of return migration and education: Transnational duties in migratory processes. *Journal of Global Ethics*, 14(1), 54–70.

Galda, L. (1998). Mirrors and windows: Reading as transformation. In T. E. Raphael & K. H. Au (Eds.), *Literature-based instruction: Reshaping the curriculum* (pp. 1–11). ERIC.

Gándara, P. (2016). Policy report: The students we share. *Mexican Studies* 32(2): 357–378. doi:10.1525/mex.2016.32.2.357.

Gándara, P., & Jensen, B. (2021). *The students we share: Preparing US and Mexican teachers for our transnational future*. SUNY Press.

García, O., Johnson, S., & Seltzer, K. (2017). *The translanguaging classroom: Leveraging student bilingualism for learning*. Caslon.

Hamann, E. T., & Zúñiga, V. (2011). Schooling, national affinity(ies), and transnational students in Mexico. In S. Vandeyar (Ed.), *Hyphenated selves: Immigrant identities within education contexts*. Rozenburg Publishers, UNISA.

Hamann, E. T., & Zúñiga, V. (2021). What educators in Mexico and in the U.S. need to know and acknowledge to attend to the educational needs of transnational students. In

P. Gándara & B. Jensen (Eds.), *The students we share: Preparing US and Mexican teachers for our transnational future* (pp. 99–117). SUNY Press.

Hamann, E. T., Zúñiga, V., & Sánchez García, J. (Eds.). (forthcoming). *Lo que los maestros de México necesitan conocer sobre la educación básica en las escuelas de Estados Unidos*. Universidad Pedagógica Nacional.

Hamann, T., Zúñiga, V., & López López, Y. A. (2020). Why the trauma, identity, and language (TIDAL) framework applies in Baja, California. AERA 2020, online.

Hanushek, E. A. (2016). What matters for student achievement. *Education Next*, 16(2), 19–26.

Henderson, T. J. (2011). *Beyond borders: A history of Mexican migration to the United States* (Vol. 13). John Wiley & Sons.

Jefferies, J., & Dabach, D. B. (2014). Breaking the silence: Facing undocumented issues in teacher practice. *Association of Mexican American Educators Journal*, 8(1).

Kemmeter, P. (2005). *El Muro/The Wall*. Entrelibros.

Kibler, A. G., Valdés, G., & Walqui A. (Eds.). (2021). *Reconceptualizing the role of critical dialogue in American classrooms: Promoting equity through dialogic education*. Routledge.

Kleyn, T. (Ed.). (n.d.). Una vida, dos Países: Children and youth (back) in Mexico/ Niños y jóvenes (de regreso) en México: The curriculum/El currículo. www.unavidathefilm.com.

Kleyn, T. & The New Dreamer del CETis 124. (Ed.) (2015). Guía de apoyo a docentes con estudiantes transfronterizos: alumnos de educación básica y media superior. www.tatyanakleyn.com/guides.

Kleyn, T. & López, D. (2021). Teaching current immigration issues to secondary immigrant and U.S.-born students: Interdisciplinary dialogic learning for critical understandings. In A. Kibler, G. Valdés, & A. Walqui (Eds.), *Reconceptualizing the role of critical dialogue in American classrooms: Promoting equity through dialogic education* (pp 132–156). Routledge.

Kleyn. T., Perez, W. & Vásquez, R. (2016). Una vida, dos países: Children and youth (back) in Mexico [Documentary]. www.unavidathefilm.com.

Lainez, R. C. (2017). *Mamá the alien/Mamá la extraterrestre*. Lee & Low Books.

Lukes, M. (2015). *Latino immigrant youth and interrupted schooling: Dropouts, dreamers and alternative pathways to college*. Multilingual Matters.

Menken, K., & Sánchez, M. T. (2019). Translanguaging in English-only schools: From pedagogy to stance in the disruption of monolingual policies and practices. *TESOL Quarterly*, 53(3), 741–767.

Morales A., & Uribe, L. (2021). *Areli is a dreamer: A true story*. Penguin Random House.

Meyers, S. V. (2014). *Del otro lado: Literacy and migration across the U.S.-Mexico border*. Southern Illinois University Press.

Meyer, P. J., & Taft-Morales, M. (2019). Central American migration: Root causes and US policy. *Congressional Research Service*, 27.

Nieto, S. (2009). *Language, culture, and teaching: Critical perspectives*. Routledge.

Otros Dreams en Acción (n.d.). About us. www.odamexico.org.

Paris, D., & Alim, H. S. (Eds.). (2017). *Culturally sustaining pedagogies: Teaching and learning for justice in a changing world*. Teachers College Press.

Tacelosky, K. (2013). Community-based service-learning as a way to meet the linguistic needs of transnational students in Mexico. *Hispania*, 96(2), 328–341.

Urrieta, L. (2013). Familia and comunidad-based saberes: Learning in an Indigenous heritage community. *Anthropology & Education Quarterly*, 44(3), 320–335.

Valenzuela, A. (1999). *Subtractive schooling: US–Mexican youth and the politics of caring*. Teachers College Press.

Vega, L. A. A. (2019). *López Obrador's initial policies toward Central American migrants: Implications for the US*. Center for the United States and Mexico, Rice University's Baker Institute for Public Policy.

Velasco, P. (2010). Indigenous students in bilingual Spanish–English classrooms in New York: a teacher's mediation strategies. *International Journal of the Sociology of Language*, 206, 255–271. doi:10.1515/IJSL.2010.057.

Verza, M. (2020, January 18). Mexico blocks hundreds of migrants from crossing border span. AP. https://apnews.com/article/8670e80d374a20d15f30bcb50d6adb6a.

Zúñiga, V., & Hamann, E.T. (2008). Escuelas nacionales, alumnos transnacionales: La migración México–Estados Unidos como fenómeno escolar. *Estudios Sociológicos de El Colegio de México*, 26(76): 65–85.

EPILOGUE

Where Are They Now?

The qualitative data for this book were collected in 2014 and the photographs were taken from 2014–2020. Since the start of the study there have been major changes in the students' lives, within and across borders. Here we provide a brief update on most of the transborder students and their families, along with more recent photographs of them over five years after the study began.[1]

Elementary Students

Melany continues to live with her family in Ciénaga de Zimatlán where she is attending her last year of secundaria, or 9th grade. When she's not in school she likes to walk her dogs Akela, Muñeca, and Nachoor and create videos to post on TikTok. Her parents hope that she will go to college and then decide on a career that will be good for her. Melany would like to be an actress and live in Los Angeles when she grows up.

Zayd, the youngest of Alberta's three children, had graduated from primaria (6th grade), and Axianeydt and Karla were in secundaria in Ciénaga de Zimatlán, when the three siblings moved to New York City to live with their father in July 2019. Axianeydt is currently in 10th grade, Karla in 9th, and Zayd in 8th (albeit via online virtual schooling due to the COVID-19 pandemic). Alberta continues to live in her parents' home in Ciénaga. She is studying law and works part-time in retail in downtown Oaxaca.

DOI: 10.4324/9780429340178-11

FIGURE E.1 Axianeydt, with her sister, Karla, and brother, Zayd, behind her, wait for a subway train in New York City (2019).

FIGURE E.2 Zayd, wearing a mask even before the coronavirus pandemic, rests on a rock in Central Park in New York after a busy day of touring the city (2019).

Epilogue 163

FIGURE E.3 Karla, left, Axianeydt, their father, and Zayd in New York City (2019).

FIGURE E.4 Alberta, working in Oaxaca, selling belts and other accessories, at the downtown street stand she set up in order to pay for law school (2019).

Secondary Students

Sharely graduated from high school in Oaxaca and then studied for one semester at the Universidad Autónoma Benito Juárez de Oaxaca before deciding to end her studies and begin working. She lives in San Juan Guelavía with her parents. She teaches English to local schoolchildren and works as a part-time translator. Nancy, Sharely's younger US-born sister, graduated from secundaria (9th grade) in Oaxaca in July 2020, then moved to Southern California, where she lives with a friend of her parents and attends high school.

FIGURE E.5 Nancy, center, with her mom, left, and Sharely, outside of their house in San Juan Guelavía (2019).

> At that moment [this photograph was taken] I didn't even imagine that I would be studying far from my family, and maybe for many years ... Now, I think of those moments when they were at my side, knowing they cared for me whether I do well or not. I was with my family. And that is the best. Now, I am not with them, but I know I will always have them present in me, every smell, taste, sight, words, and reactions I have. I am thankful for all the tiring weeks my parents dedicated to me.
>
> —Nancy

Melchor graduated high school and was accepted into a private college to study tourism. Due to the high cost of tuition, he was unable to attend and started working instead. He has held a number of jobs including selling cell phones, factory work, and is currently giving bilingual tours at a local mezcal distributor. He has also begun experimenting with photography. Melchor has taken on a larger role supporting his family after his father was in an accident, which he is recovering from. But he feels ready for this added responsibility.

Tertiary Students

Erik completed the coursework for the language education program at the UABJO, but didn't receive the bachelor's degree due to additional requirements and bureaucratic processes. As a result, he never worked as a teacher. Instead he worked in the family business running a small recreational center in their home-town and also had jobs in a restaurant and hostel, where his English came in handy. Then he decided to make the journey back to the US once again. He crossed the Mexico–US border and is back in New Jersey, where he works in landscaping with his older brother.

Yauzin graduated with a bachelor's degree in language education. She taught English to elementary school children for three years. Then she went on to teach undergraduate students English at the UABJO, her alma mater. Since being back in Oaxaca she has traveled to the US on four different occasions (she was hoping to have gone a fifth time, but COVID-19 changed those plans). Yauzin purchased a plot of land 20 minutes outside the city of Oaxaca where she is planning to build her own home.

FIGURE E.6 During Yauzin's last trip to the US, she reunited in New York City's Central Park with Zayd, Karla, and Axianeydt, (front and center), who had arrived in NYC a month earlier. Yauzin got together with City University of New York (CUNY) alumni who were part of a study abroad trip to Oaxaca, for which Yauzin was a teaching assistant. From left to right in the back row: Yatziri, Sabrina, Yauzin, Nancy, Antonio, and Tatyana Kleyn (2019).

Note

1 Unfortunately, I was unable to contact Brayan and Ricardo for an update.

INDEX

Page numbers in italics refer to figures. Page numbers in bold refer to tables. Page numbers followed by 'n' refer to notes.

9/11 attacks 11, 75

admissions policies/practices 115–117
agency of students 56–60
Alberta *34*, 35, *47*, 56, 77, *79*, *82*, *113*, 161, *163*; on cost of education 133; on dual citizenship 81–83; and family unification 47; passports for US-born children of 80
Alberto 48, *58*, *74*
Alfredo *48*
American-Mexican children 14
Anderson, Jill 146
anti-immigrant policies 4, 12–13, 53, 58, 147
Antonio 53, 75, 95, 96–97
Anzaldúa, Gloria 7, 8, 64, 65, 71, 74, 85–86
apostille 115–116, 117
Arizona Senate Bill 1070 11
artifacts, student 3, 23, 67–70, *67*, *68*, *69*, 83, *83*, 84, *84*
asylum seekers 6
Axianeydt *21*, 34, 35, *36*, *47*, 81, *101*, *113*, *123*, *134*, 161, *162*, *163*, *166*; anime drawings 84, *84*; drawing of Mexico and US 68–69, *68*; and family unification 47, *48*; images of home 68–69; schooling experiences of 124; use of English 100–101

Baquedano-López, P. 14
belonging, sense of 78, 84
Biden, Joe 11
bilingual education 150; intercultural 92; and Mexican student diversity 156; in Mexico 119–120; in United States 97, 118–119
binational children 14
binational teacher education programs 120–121, 149
Bokova, I. 150
Bracero Program 8, 29, 56
Brayan 37, 98; agency of 57; on discrimination 52; and financial hardships 50; and mixed-status family experiences 76–77; schooling experiences of 124; use of English 99; view on Zapotec 92
Buttigieg, Pete 95

car culture 51
Castro, Julián 95
Cathedral of Our Lady of the Assumption, Oaxaca 25
centralized education system 112
CETis (Centro de Estudios Tecnológicos, Industrial y de Servicios) 31, 93–94, 153
children's literature 151–152
Chinese Exclusion Act of 1882 9
Ciénega de Zimatlán 27–29, *28*

168 Index

citizenship: cultural 65, 76, 78, 85; doble nacionalidad/dual citizenship 37, 81–83, 85, 135, 145; global 150; hierarchies of 52; and mixed-status families 76; national 65; *vs.* nationality 65; naturalization 65, 71; political 71, 72, 76, 78, 85; price of US citizenship rights 79–81; strategic 81
Clinton, Bill 10
coercion, and return migration 12–13
college students *see* tertiary students
community obligations 54–56
complex personhood 75–76
compulsory education 112
Constitución Política de los Estados Unidos Mexicanos 65
Cortez Román, N. A. 129
crimmigration 11, 75
Cristopher 37, 76, 77
critical dialogic education 151
Cruz-Manjarrez, A. 14
cultural brokers 99
cultural citizenship 65; and mixed-status families 76, 78; of secondary students 85
culturally sustaining pedagogy 156–157
CUNY-Initiative on Immigration and Education (CUNY-IIE) 152, 158n2
cyclical/circular migration 7–8, 14, 15–16, 144

decentralized education system 112
Deferred Action for Childhood Arrivals (DACA) 40, 78–79
Délano Alonso, A. 8, 145
deportations 10, 11, 12, 53, 106n2
deservingness 10
Development, Relief, Education for Alien Minors Act *see* DREAM Act
Día de los Muertos (Day of the Dead) 25, 35
discrimination 52, 53, 90–91
doble nacionalidad/dual citizenship 37, 81–83, 85, 135, 145
drawings of elementary students 67–70, 67, 68, 69, 84, 84
DREAM Act 10
Dream Teams 152
dual citizenship *see* doble nacionalidad/dual citizenship

economic freedom 50
education 110–111, 148; admissions policies/practices 115–117; advocacy 126–128; bilingual education/TESOL programs in US 118–119; binational teacher education programs 120–121; centralized *vs.* decentralized systems 112; college entry and major selections 128–130; comparison across levels 133–136; compulsory 112; differences in parent-child connection 124–125; and economic factors 82; higher education systems 117; intercultural bilingual education 92; language learning programs 117–121; public school language support programs and resources in 119–120; school closings 113–114; school days 112–113; schooling experiences between US and Mexico 123–125; structures, across countries 111–117; student composition 114–115; transborder students becoming English language teachers 130–132; transnational higher education plans 132–133; views and experiences of Mexican teachers/teacher educators 121–123; *see also* higher education; pedagogy
elementary students **33**, 34–36, 161; agency of 56, 60; Ciénega de Zimatlán 27–29, 28; drawings 67–70, 67, 68, 69, 84, 84; dual citizenship of 81, 85; education of 134–135; English learning of 98–99; and external perceptions/questions 72; higher education plans of 133; identities of 85; images of home 67–70; languaging experiences of 105; link between language and national identities 70; schooling experiences of 124; use of English 100–101
Emanuel 35–36, 56; on dual citizenship 81, 82; and financial hardships 49–50; on higher education costs 133; on mobility 51
Emergency Medical Treatment and Active Labor Act of 1986 51
employment 8, 48, 99
English 98–99; communication of teachers with transborder students in 122; grammar 102–103, 132; growth, creative approaches to 154; informal tutoring by transborder students 123; as a killer language 99–100; "long term English learners" 104; in schools 102–104; teachers, transborder students becoming 130–132; views across and within borders 99–101

Index   169

Erik 40–41, 42, *83*, 98, 165; agency of 58; in English language program 131–132; English skills of 102; ESL programs 118, 119; and religious traditions 54, 55–56; and soccer 83–84
ESL programs 118–119
Español *see* Spanish/Español
Espindola, J. 144, 148
Estefana 114
European Union 143–144
E-Verify program 11
exclusion 52
experts by experience 39
Ezpeleta, J. 113

Facultad de Idiomas (Faculty of Languages) 32, 129, 131
family unification 46–49
Feliciano 51–52, 89
financial hardships 48, 49–51
Formadores de Docentes Binacionales (FBD) 120–121
freedom 4, 50, 73, 74–75, 124
free will, and return migration 13
Fundación SM México, La 130

Galda, L. 157
Galván, R. T. 133–134
gendered wages 49–51
General Law of the Linguist Rights of Indigenous Peoples (2003), Mexico 117–118
gentrification 97
global citizenship, education for 150
global migration 5–6
Gonzalez, L. 8
grammar skills, English 102–103, 132
Guelaguetza 25, 29
Guía de apoyo a docentes con estudiantes transfronterizos: alumnos de educación básica y media superior (Kleyn & The New Dreamer del CETis 124) 153

Hamann, E. T. 120, 129, 152
Hanushek, E. A. 149
Harpaz, Y. 81
health insurance 51
Heidbrink, L. 39
Henderson, T. J. 141–142
Herminia 40, 96, 115
Hierve el Agua *4*
higher education 39; access to 12, 52–53, 79, 117, 128–129; college entry and

major selections 128–130; cost of 133; faculty 121; financial aid 82; selection of major 129; systems 117; transnational higher education plans 132–133
high school students *see* secondary students
home, images of 66–70
House Bill 4400, South Carolina 53
hyperpolicing 52

identities 64–65; comparison across levels 85–86; DACA 78–79; doble nacionalidad/dual citizenship 81–83; and dualities 64; external perceptions and questions 71–73; images of home 66–70; internalization of undocumented immigrant identity in United States 73–76; language as basis for national identities 70–71; mixed-status families 76–79; national 64; price of US citizenship rights 79–81; and sports 83–84
Illegal Immigration Reform and Immigration Responsibility Act (IIRIRA) 10, 59
immigrant justice school clubs 152
immigration 9–10; crimmigration 11, 75; equitable policy 147; issues, integrating into teacher certification 155; reforms 10, 11, 147; right to circulate 144, 147
Immigration and Customs Enforcement (ICE) 11, 12, 75, 146–147
immigration courts 12
immigration detention: abolishing 146–147; centers 13, 147
Immigration Reform and Control Act (IRCA) 10
Indigenous knowledge 154
Indigenous languages 154, 156; *see also* Zapotec
Instituto Oaxaqueño de Atención al Migrante (IOAM) 23, 27, 145
Instituto para las Mujeres en la Migración (IMUMI) 115
instructional time 113
intercultural bilingual education 92
internal migration 5–6
international migrant children 14
interviews 23
invisible bars 51

Jacobo-Suárez, M. 144, 148
Jezreel *34*, 35

170 Index

Jong-Min 51
Juárez, A. M. A. 29

Karla *21*, 34, 35, *36*, *45*, *47*, *71*, *79*, *82*, *101*, 161, *162*, *163*, *166*; drawing of Mexico and US *69*, 70; and external perceptions/questions 72; and family unification 47; images of home 70; schooling experiences of 124; use of English 100

language 81, 88–90; as basis for national identities 70–71; comparison across levels 105–106; and discrimination against Indigenous peoples 90–91; English 98–104; Indigenous 154, 156; language learning programs 117–118; languaging 89; and political identity 71; practices of transborder students, partial/racialized views of 104–105; Spanish (Español) 94–98; translanguaging 89, 95, 98, 104; and undocumented status in United States 96–97; Zapotec 90–94
Lau v. Nichols (1974) 117, 118, 122
legal permanent residents (LPRs) 106n2
Leidy 36, 46, 49, 50, 56
Lillehaugen, Brook Danielle 94
long-term health care, access to 51–52
López, Dina 151
Lopez, Felipe H. 94
López-Gopar, M. E. 100, 103, 121, 128, 131
Lo que los maestros de México necesitan conocer sobre la educación básica en las escuelas de Estados Unidos (Hamann) 153
Loredo, Maggie 146

Margarita *48*, *91*
Maria *45*
Martha 50–51
Mateos, P. 81
mayordomía 54–56
Melany 35–36, 97, 161; agency of 56; bilingual education 118; drawing of Mexico and US *67*, 68; images of home 68; link between language and national identities 70
Melchor 37, 165; access to long-term health care 51; advocacy 126–127, 128; agency of 57; family, Zapotec use in 90; on high school English classes 102; identity of 64; language practices 89; on school fees 112; undocumented

immigrant identity of 73; use of English 99, 100; use of Spanish 95; view on Zapotec 92
metalinguistic knowledge 103
Mexican–US War 7
Mexico: admissions policies/practices in 115–117; centralized education system 112; citizenship 65, 81; college entry in 128–129; compulsory education in 112; cost of higher education in 133; costs of schooling in 112; efforts for reduce shortage of English teachers 130; higher education system in 117; map of *26*; Mexico–US–Mexico cyclical migration demographics 15–16; policies, and pedagogies 152–154; policies promoting out-migration from 8–9; policy recommendations for 145–146; protests against educational reforms in 42; public school language support programs and resources in 119–120; school days in 112–113; schooling experiences in 124–125; student composition in 114, 115; US–Mexico border 6–7, 144; views and experiences of teachers/teacher educators in 121–123
migration 5, 142; cyclical/circular 7–8, 14, 15–16, 144; global 5–6; internal 5; out-migration policies 8–12; seasonal migrants 27; support for migrants from Mexican consulates 145; teaching through multimodal resources about 151–152; undocumented immigrants 6, 8, 10, 11–12
Miguel *21*
mixed-status families 37, 76–79, 85, 153
mobility, and economic opportunity 51
multilateral agreements 149

Nancy 38, *39*, *58*, *63*, 74, 77, *91*, *125*, *141*, 164, *164*
national borders, deregulation of 143–144
national citizenship 65
national identities 64; external perceptions and questions 72; language as basis for 70–71
national policies 144–147
naturalization 65, 71
Nepantla 85–86
networks, and migration 29
New Dreamers 37, 152, 153
new returnees 14

Index **171**

New York State Youth Leadership Council (NYSYLC) 152
non-governmental organizations, funding of 146
North American Free Trade Agreement (NAFTA) 8–9

Oaxaca 25, 27, 95; Ciénega de Zimatlán 27–29, *28*; fiesta patronal *55*, 56; school closings in 113–114; Tlacolula de Matamoros 30–31, *30*; Universidad Autónoma Benito Juárez de Oaxaca 31–33
Obama, Barack 40, 78
Ong, A. 65
Otros Dreams en Acción (ODA) 130, 146
out-migration: from Mexico, policies promoting 8–9; from United States, policies promoting 9–12
out-of-state tuition fees 12, 53, 128

passports 80
Patel, L. 10
pedagogy 142, 148; awareness of Mexican student diversity 155–156; bilingual programs 150; building awareness of transborder students 153; creating spaces for Indigenous languages 156; critical dialogic education 151; culturally sustaining 156–157; education for global citizenship 150; immigrant justice school clubs 152; inclusion of Indigenous language/knowledge 154; integrating immigration issues into teacher certification 155; Mexican policies and 152–154; multilateral agreements 149; professional development for teachers 153; Spanish support classes 153–154; teacher preparation and education shifts 149–150; teaching migration through multimodal resources 151–152; transnational policies and 149–152; United States policies and 154–157; *see also* education
Peña Nieto, Enrique 42
photo-elicitation method 24
photography 24–25
Plyler v. Doe (1982) 115, 147
Poch@House 146
policies 142–143; abolishing ICE and immigration detention 146–147; increased rights for undocumented immigrants 147; large-scale

regularization and circulation 147; Mexican 144–146, 152–154; non-governmental organization funding 146; pedagogy 148–157; poverty reduction measures 145; promoting out-migration 8–12; reacclimation support 145; transnational 143–144, 149–152, 158n1; United States 146–147, 154–157; *see also* pedagogy
political citizenship 72; of elementary students 85; and language 71; and mixed-status families 76, 78; of secondary students 85
Poughkeepsie, New York 29
poverty reduction measures 145
professional development for teachers 153
Programa Nacional de Inglés (PRONI) 102

racism 52, 53
reacclimation support 145
Reagan, Ronald 10
Reforma Educativa 114
refugees 6
refusal, and return migration 13
religious traditions 54–56
remittances 8, 29, 31, 43n3
research methodology 22–25
returnees/retornados 14
return migrants 14
return migration 3–4, 6; categories of 12–13, *12*; demographics of 15–16; terminology 14–15
Ricardo 41–42; agency of 57–58; English skills of 102; and external perceptions/questions 72; schooling experiences of 124; selection of major 129
rights: right to circulate 144, 147; of undocumented immigrants 147; US citizenship, price of 79–81

safety nets 145
Sánchez García, J. 120
school closings 113–114
school days 112–113
seasonal migrants 27
secondary students *33*, 36–38, 164–165; and advocacy 126–127, 128; agency of 57, 59; education of 135; and English classes in Mexico 102, 120; higher education plans of 133; identities of 85; languaging experiences of 105–106; learning of Zapotec 94; link between language and national identities 70; and

172 Index

mixed-status family experiences 76–78; schooling experiences of 125; Tlacolula de Matamoros 30–31, *30*; undocumented immigrant identity of 73, 74; use of English 98–100; use of Spanish 95; views on Zapotec 92–93

Secretaría de Educación Pública, La (SEP) 115–116 120

self, sense of 64, 78, 106, 142

service learning projects 154

Sharely 38, *38*, *39*, 52, *58*, *63*, *74*, *88*, *91*, *93*, 112, *125*, *141*, 164, *164*; advocacy 127–128; agency of 57, 59; on composition of peers 114; English tutoring experience of 102; experience of undocumented immigrant status 73, 74; family, Zapotec use in 90; and family unification 47, *48*; link between language and national identities 70; and mixed-status family experiences 77–78; notion of home *66*; schooling experiences of 125; use of English 99; view on Zapotec 92–93

"show-me-your-papers" law 11

siblings of secondary students 34, 35, 76–78, 81, 85

soccer 83–84

Spanglish 95

Spanish/Español 95; in schools 97–98; support classes 153–154; US-based Spanish practices 97; use within and across borders 95–97; writing in 97–98

special education teachers 122

strategic citizenship 81

strikes 114

student clubs 152

student composition 114–115

Students with Limited or Interrupted Formal Education (SLIFE) 155

Stumpf, J. 75

Sughrua, W. 100

teacher(s): bilingual 150; binational teacher education programs 120–121, 149; certification, integrating immigration issues into 155; English language, transborder students becoming 130–132; leveraging English skills of transborder students 102; Mexican, views and experiences of 121–123; preparation 149–150; professional development for

153–154; special education 122; unions 42, 113–114

Tere 38, *58*, 77–78, 124–125

tertiary students **33**, 39–42, 165; access to higher education 53–54, 129; and advocacy 126; agency of 57–59; education of 135–136; English skills of 102; and external perceptions/questions 72–73; higher education plans of 132–133; identities of 83–84, 85; language practices of 95–96; languaging experiences of 106; and mixed-status family experiences 78–79; schooling experiences of 124; selection of major 129; sharing of US and English experiences 101; and Spanish writing 98; undocumented immigrant identity of 75; Universidad Autónoma Benito Juárez de Oaxaca 31–33; *see also* higher education

TESOL programs in United States 118–119

Tilly, C. 29

Tlacolula de Matamoros 30–31, *30*

Tony 40, 78, *96*

transborder students 14, 22; agency, in migration 56–60; building awareness of 153; Ciénega de Zimatlán 27–29, *28*; and continual change 42; and dualities 64; elementary students 34–36; secondary students 36–38; tertiary students 39–42; Tlacolula de Matamoros 30–31, *30*; Universidad Autónoma Benito Juárez de Oaxaca 31–33

transfronterizo children 14–15

translanguaging 89, 95, 98, 104

transnational children 14

transnational policies 143, 158n1; deregulation of national borders 143–144; focusing on most vulnerable countries/groups 144; and pedagogies 149–152

transportation 35, 51

Trato de Libre Comercio (TLC) *see* North American Free Trade Agreement (NAFTA)

travel, cross-border 76–77, 79

Treaty of Guadalupe Hidalgo (1848) 7, 52

Trump, Donald 11

Una Vida, Dos Países: Children and Youth (Back) in Mexico 23, 151, 152

uniforms 124

union activism, impact on schooling 114

Index **173**

United National Human Rights Commission (UNHCR) 6
United States (US): admissions policies/practices in 115; bilingual education and TESOL programs in 118–119; citizenship 65; college entry in 128, 129; compulsory education in 112; decentralized education system of 112; higher education system in 117; internalization of undocumented immigrant identity in 73–76; language learning programs in 117; Mexico–US–Mexico cyclical migration demographics 15–16; policies, and pedagogies 154–157; policies promoting out-migration from 9–12; policy recommendations for 146–147; school days in 113; schooling experiences in 124–125; student composition 114, 115; teachers unions in 114; travel of mixed-status families from Mexico to 76–77; US–Canada border 144; use of Spanish in 95; US–Mexico border 6–7, 144
Universidad Autónoma Benito Juárez de Oaxaca (UABJO) 31–33, 128, 153; entrance exam 98, 128; Indigenous language courses in 94
Universidad Pedagógica Nacional (UPN) 153
University of Dayton Publishing 130
US Citizenship and Immigration Services (USCIS) 77

Vásquez, Rafael 30, 92
Velasco, P. 156

Voces del Valle US-CETis 124 program 94
voluntary departure 13
vulnerable countries/groups, transnational policies focusing on 144

wages, gendered 49–51
Weiss, E. 113
white supremacy 9, 24, 53, 100
writing in Spanish 97–98

xenophobia 9, 53, 100

Yauzin 40–41, *40, 54, 59, 96,* 102, 110–111, *110,* 165, *166;* access to higher education 53–54, 129; advocacy 126; agency of 58–59; college enrollment process for 115–116; and DACA 78–79; on discrimination 52; as English teacher *130, 131, 148;* ESL programs 118; and external perceptions/questions 72–73; language practices of 99–100; metalinguistic knowledge of English 103; and mixed-status family experiences 78–79; selection of major 129; and Spanish learning 95–96, 98; and Spanish writing 98; undocumented immigrant identity of 75, 76

Zapotec 89, 90–91, 105; in schools 93–94; view across and within borders 91–93
Zayd 34, 35, 47, *47, 48, 79, 101,* 161, *162, 163, 166*
Zine, J. 83
Zúñiga, V. 120, 152

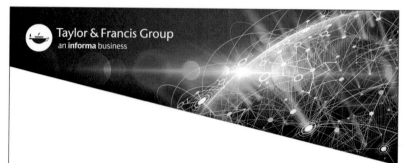